LAST FAIRY TALES

Ed Laboulaye

LAST FAIRY TALES

BY

ÉDOUARD LABOULAYE *de, 1811-1883*

AUTHORIZED TRANSLATION
BY
MARY L. BOOTH

ILLUSTRATED

JUV

Core Collection Books, inc.
GREAT NECK, NEW YORK

First Published 1884
Reprinted 1976

International Standard Book Number
0-8486-0208-0

Library of Congress Catalog Number
76-9900

PRINTED IN THE UNITED STATES OF AMERICA

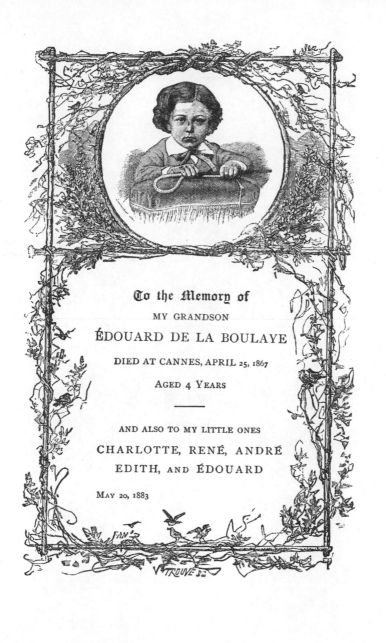

To the Memory of

MY GRANDSON

ÉDOUARD DE LA BOULAYE

DIED AT CANNES, APRIL 25, 1867

AGED 4 YEARS

———

AND ALSO TO MY LITTLE ONES

CHARLOTTE, RENÉ, ANDRÉ

EDITH, AND ÉDOUARD

MAY 20, 1883

LAST
FAIRY TALES.

AUTHOR'S PREFACE.

WHEN we were children (which was somewhere about 1820), we were presented with fairy tales at New-Year for our amusement. By whom they were written mattered little; provided they kept us still for an hour without quarrelling or breaking things, the book was thought a good one, and nothing more was asked of the author.

Since that time a great change has taken place. Fairy tales now hold a prominent place in literature. Like great noblemen, they have their pedigree and history. They treat of geography, astronomy, and zoology, and will very soon include philosophy and religion. Analysis has appeared; farewell to jollity. An ancient muse, of whom we must speak no ill, because she is a lady, and of uncertain age, and also because she is too often in the right—Science, since we must call her by her name—with her long fingers, hooked nose, and

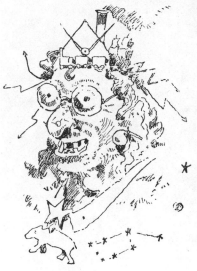

great round goggles, is prying into everything. We can no longer laugh at an ogre without being lacking in respect to the god Orcus ; Riquet with the Tuft is nothing but the Winter Solstice ; and the White Cat, in her enchanted castle, is the nymph Calisto, or, rather, the Great Bear in person. A plague on our grandnephews ; they are too wise for us old fellows !

For my part, I, too, could invent theories as well as others, if I saw fit. With the protection and support of a respectable political coterie I should stand a good chance of admission to the Academy of Mother Goose ; for I have her blood in my veins. I know what fairy tales are. I have tried to make them, and have thereby learned a great truth, namely, that these tales are not manufactured to order. The brightest man is put to his wit's end when he undertakes the task. At most, he invents some allegory as innocent as it is transparent ; he tells a story at which he himself is the first to laugh, and which does not for an instant beguile his readers, however young. I therefore hold it as a maxim that the more sense a man has, the more insipid and tedious are his fairy tales.

"But, grandpapa," says my little grandson, "your stories are very amusing."

"*Sancta simplicitas!* If my stories are amusing, as you say, it is because I did not make them, my child."

"Then who did make them, grandpapa?"

"My child, I have taken them by piecemeal from all parts, North, South, and elsewhere."

"But who invented them in the South?"

"Everybody and nobody, my young critic. A fairy tale is a story, a legend, or

an event that chances to be told of a winter's evening by some soldier or sailor, who dresses it up to suit himself, regardless of time or place. Then it is caught up by nurses and sung to children to amuse them or to serve as a lullaby, until at last some one with a poetic imagination gives it a fantastic turn, when lo! the fairy tale is brought forth. The author is nameless and unknown; the work is immortal. Who would dare claim the paternity of Cinderella and Tom Thumb?"

Stranger still, the fairy-tale has no native land, any more than it has an author. Every nation tells Little Red Riding Hood in its own fashion, and it would take a sharp critic to

discover the original text of all these versions. The canvas
is of no consequence, the embroidery is everything; and this
embroidery changes with each century.

What is Puss in Boots, for example? A good genius, in
the skin of an animal, that enriches his young master. The
idea might occur a hundred times in different countries,
trivial and insignificant as it is. Now, compare Perrault's
Puss in Boots with the version of the Pentameron, which
will be found in the present volume, with some other old
friends under new faces. Perrault was but a child when
Gianbattista Basilio died, and, in all probability, never heard
of the Neapolitan tales. Yet here is the same story told in

two different countries. The idea is the same, and the details resemble each other ; but what a difference there is between the two stories! With Perrault the work is fantastic, the result of a cat's caprice. With Basilio it is a moral tale, designed as a lesson to ingrates. And now, where is the primitive story to be found? Perchance it may yet be discovered in India ; but we may be sure that it will have been so often retold and transformed on its way that it can only be discerned by the sharp eye of an expert in fairy lore.

ÉDOUARD LABOULAYE.

PARIS, 1883.

TRANSLATOR'S PREFACE.

THIS compilation contains all the fairy tales written by
the lamented Édouard Laboulaye, that prince of story-tell-
ers and most eloquent of statesmen, from the publication of
his Fairy Book, several years ago, to the time of his death,
last year. The brilliant Professor of the Institute of France,
whose lively sympathy during the late civil war won him
our country's love and gratitude, found recreation from his
graver labors in narrating these fanciful stories, overflowing
with wit and humor, which delighted both old and young,
and this task he continued to his dying day, the preface to
the volume containing part of the tales found herein being his last work, and the touching dedication to his little
grandchildren bearing date only five days before his death.

M. Laboulaye always delighted in seeing his writings in
an English dress, and took keen pleasure in the interest and
appreciation of his American readers. This translation is
made with his authorization, and the subsequent kind ap-
proval of his family. Death alone prevented him from

furnishing to this volume, as he did to the last, a preface especially addressed to American children. It is sad to think that these pages will never meet his kindly eye, and that the pen which had⋅ such power to charm is laid aside forever.

Those who remember the publication by Harper & Brothers of that sparkling collection of stories, Laboulaye's Fairy Book, know what a *furore* it created, not only among the children, who were fascinated with its giants, fairies, and hobgoblins, but still more among their elders, who were charmed with the flashing wit and keen satire which leavened every page, and which, to the writer's personal knowledge, beguiled the Vice-President of the United States, as well as the president of one of our largest banking institutions, into sitting up nearly all night to finish the volume.

The present collection is even richer, wittier, and more varied than its predecessor. It is compiled from the different works of M. Laboulaye, and contains all the children's tales not included in the first Fairy Book. And what a wealth is there of fantastic stories of enchantments that rival the Arabian Nights, together with delightful apologues, and old tales retold with a bewitching humor that gives them a new charm, all narrated with a purity and high moral tone that make them safe as well as amusing reading for the young! Children will be enchanted with this new Fairy Book, which is sure to hold a lasting place in their affections for this and succeeding generations. But the truest appreciation, after all, of this witty volume will come from the adults, who, as they laugh at its diverting sallies, will breathe a sigh in memory of the author, and rejoice at the opportunity to lay a leaf on the grave of one of the most ardent friends of our Union in its hour of peril.

Mention should be made of the very lavish manner in which the volume is illustrated, which makes it a genuine picture-book. It is literally crammed with nearly three hundred spirited drawings by the brilliant French artists, Henri Pillé, Henri Manesse, Yan' Dargent, and the lately deceased Henri Scott, some of whose last designs are here included.

MARY L. BOOTH.

NEW YORK, 1884.

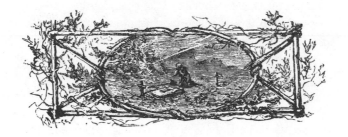

CONTENTS.

xviii   *Contents.*

THE THREE WONDERS
OF THE WORLD.

I.

ONCE upon a time there was a queen who had three sons. The eldest was named Prince Lofty; the second, Prince Reckless; and the third, Prince Prosper. All three were as beautiful as the day; all three adored their mother; and all three took the greatest delight in forestalling her wishes and doing her will. The queen must have been very happy, one would suppose. She was, as a mother, but not as a woman. She was a prey to a malady which none of us can escape, and which is called old age. When she looked in the mirror, the horrible grimness which years had stamped upon her

face made her turn pale with dread. Her white hair, her
wrinkled forehead, her toothless gums, and her watery eyes
all told her that she must die.

The poor queen was terribly afraid of death. She could
not be resigned to quit her children, her throne, and her
people. Her sons sought in vain to comfort her; the more
they loved her, the less courage she had to bid them an eternal farewell.

One day they heard, I know not how, that the King of the Bitter Waters had a wonderful bird, whose warbling renewed the youth of those over whose heads it sung. The most marvellous tales were told concerning this peerless songster. One day, it was said, a minister of state, ninety years old, who chanced to pass under the tree where this marvel was singing, instantly became rejuvenated to such a degree that he had to be carried away in a nurse's arms. What would not the good queen have given to hear these heavenly songs, had she been made only twenty or thirty years younger thereby !

The three brothers consulted together. The eldest insisted on being the first to go in search of this wonderful bird. The queen refused her consent. "It is for you, my children," she said, "that I wish to live. If one of you should perish in this undertaking, nothing would be left me but to die. Stay with me, and let God's will be done !"

Prince Lofty, however, was not one to be dismayed. Taking a good horse, arms, and money, he told his brothers that if he did not return within a year they might know that he was dead or a prisoner, embraced his mother, and set out on his way. He went straight onward till he reached the city where dwelt the happy owner of the wonderful bird. Here he found an inn, and inquired what truth there was in the story.

"All you have heard is true," answered the host, "but the whole truth has not been told you. The King of the Bitter Waters is a treacherous and cruel magician. No one who has entered his palace has ever come out again. If you have kindred and friends, handsome youth, do not attempt a perilous enterprise, in which you will succeed no better than those who have gone before you."

Lofty thanked the host, put his horse in the stable, supped

heartily, went to bed, and had the most delightful dreams. Early the next morning he repaired to the king's palace. The door was wide open ; neither guards nor servants were to be seen. Lofty mounted the staircase without meeting any one, pushed open a door, and entered a vast hall, surrounded with marble statues of helmeted knights of all nations, vizors down and swords in hand. · In the middle of the hall were hundreds of cages with the most beautiful birds imaginable. One of these, all of gold, especially struck the prince's eye. "That must be the wonderful bird," thought he. He called aloud, and knocked at all the doors, but no one answered. Then, without thinking of harm, he approached the golden cage and thrust his hand into it, upon which a bell rang. One of the statues descended from its pedestal, advanced slowly towards the young man, and touched him with the point of his sword, when, lo ! Lofty was turned into a statue.

II.

One month, two months, passed away, the year finished its course, and the queen had no news of her son. Consumed with grief, she wept without ceasing, saying over and over she had sent her son to his death. The two brothers were no less grieved than their mother. Reckless went to the queen and said, "Do not weep, dear mother. I am going in search of Lofty, who is doubtless a prisoner. You may be sure that I shall soon bring him back to you, with the wonderful bird into the bargain."

The unhappy queen vainly entreated her son to stay with her ; the prince's honor forbade him to listen to counsels or prayers. Furnished with a good horse and a well-filled purse, he set out and went straight onward until he reached the same inn where his elder brother had stopped. It was

"He entered a vast hall, surrounded with marble statues."

in vain that the host lavished advice upon him ; this was not the time to think of prudence. Reckless hastened to the deserted palace, mounted the staircase, entered the great hall, and was about to lay hold of the bird, when the bell rang, the statue descended from its pedestal and touched him as it had his brother ; and, lo ! he, too, was enchanted.

III.

One month, two months passed away, the year finished its course, and the queen had no news of her two sons. She was plunged in grief, and longed to die. Prosper fell on his knees. " Do not despair, dear mother," he cried. " Let me go and I will succeed. I am sure that I shall soon bring back both my brothers and the wonderful bird."

" You shall not go, my child," said the poor queen, bathed in tears ; "you surely would not add to my sorrow and remorse. If you forsake me, what will become of me, with no one to close my eyes ?"

But Prosper kissed her hands so tenderly and made her such fair promises that she was forced to let him go. He equipped himself like his brothers, and took with him a sword that had been left in his cradle by his fairy godmother, a friend of the family, whom he had never since seen.

He set out on his journey, followed the fatal road, reached the city of the King of the Bitter Waters, stopped at the inn, and at daybreak went to the deserted palace. On entering the great hall, he saluted the green bird that was hopping about behind its golden bars, then called aloud. No one answered. He drew his sword and approached the cage. The bell rang, and the statue descended from its pedestal, sword in hand ; but the prince was beforehand with his enemy, and dealt his weapon such a blow that the stone was splintered in pieces.

The statue uttered a cry, and paused. A second knight descended from his pedestal and was received in the same way. A third and fourth met the like fate. At this moment a door opened, and a host of soldiers entered, in the midst of which was the king in person. He was a fat, little old man, with a huge turban on his head, and an enormous scimitar in his hand, which he wielded with difficulty. In a shrill voice, which he vainly tried to swell, he addressed the young prince. "Who gave you permission to enter my royal palace? Were you not told that no'one ever quits this hall alive?"

"I knew it well," answered Prosper. "If I have confronted death, great prince, it was not to brave your power. It was through love of my mother. She is old, and yonder bird can restore her youth. Before touching its cage I knocked at all the doors ; I am not a robber, and respect the property of others. I wished to offer a large sum for this wonder of the world, but could obtain no answer. How then am I to blame? O king, if you have a mother whom you love, be indulgent to me for her sake. Fix the price of this bird yourself, and all that I have, my life even, is yours."

The king burst out laughing. "Young man," he said, "you are a simpleton. Do you take me for a bird-seller? I might put you to death, but I pity you. I like courage, and your filial love touches my heart. If you wish for the bird, I will put you in the way of obtaining it. Two days' journey from here dwells my rival, the King of the Green Isles, who has a daughter whose beauty eclipses any ever beheld, whence she is called The Fairest of the Fair. This treasure the King of the Green Isles guards with jealous care. Find her, carry her off, and bring her here, and I will give you the green bird in exchange for your conquest. If you are satisfied with the bargain, set out instantly. You

"He was a fat, little old man, with a huge turban on his head."

may leave the castle ; but remember that if you dare to return empty-handed you will perish, like all before you."

IV.

Prosper, with his heart full of hope, accepted the king's
conditions, and immediately set out on his way.   After two
days' journey he reached the shore of a sea as blue as the
heavens, interspersed with islands planted with tall green
trees, which rose from the waters like great clumps of verdure.   At the west was the royal island, the residence of the
princess.   Prosper hastened thither, already promising himself the victory, but his joy was of short duration.

In a meadow, surrounded with poplars which trembled at
the lightest breeze, was a lake as smooth as a mirror.   From
the midst of this lake rose a tower a hundred feet high, without doors or windows, made of a single sheet of glass.   In
this tower was imprisoned the Fairest of the Fair.   How it
was approached, or in what way it was entered, no one had
ever known.   It was vaguely fancied that a subterranean
passage, built under the lake, connected the tower with the
royal palace, more than a mile distant.   But no one had
ever seen such a passage, and, when it was talked of, the
good people in the neighborhood shook their heads.   According to them, the tower was enchanted, and opened at
night at the sound of a magical word which was known to
the king alone.   And this secret was well guarded, for the
prince knew to a certainty that the fate of his kingdom was
bound up with that of this crystal donjon.   An oracle had
foretold that on the day his daughter quitted the prison
the tower would sink beneath the waters, carrying with it
the beautiful kingdom of the Green Isles, with all its inhabi-
tants.

Prosper skirted the lake slowly, carefully noting the tower
1*

which glistened in the midday light like a topaz in the sun's rays. The walk was a long one ; it took the prince more than five hours to return to the place from which he started. The day was closing ; the tower, colored by the setting sun, changed to a ruby tint. Weary with the journey and worn with anxiety, the prince alighted from his horse, seated himself on a hillock, and fell into a reverie. A distant clock struck six. Prosper raised his head, and spied a figure in white between the battlements of the tower. It was the Fairest of the Fair. The last rays of the sun gilded the fair hair of the prisoner. She leaned forward to look over the plain, and at the same moment there was heard a loud sound of men and horses. It was the princess's suitors, who were accustomed to march past at the hour she took her airing, all striving which should win a glance of her beautiful eyes.

They came from all countries. First in the procession was an Indian rajah, clad in silk and gold, with a necklace and bracelets of pearls. He half reclined in a howdah, borne by a huge elephant, buried beneath housings embroidered with precious stones. A numerous train of musicians, jugglers, and dancing-girls surrounded him on all sides, singing and dancing as they marched along. They paused before the tower, and a body of archers, armed with golden bows, let fly a shower of arrows, bearing on their points wreaths of flowers, gallant mottoes, and fireworks that blazed in the air. It was labor lost ; the arrows struck the walls of glass with a dull thud, without attracting the least notice from the princess.

Then followed a second caravan, headed by a Mantchoo prince, who came, it was said, to ask the Fairest of the Fair in marriage in behalf of the Emperor of China. The Tartar envoy, whose mustache fell to his knees, was mounted on a superb black horse, whose nostrils snorted fire. He was

"He half reclined in a howdah, borne by a huge elephant."

followed by a troop of soldiers dressed in tiger-skins, that marched proudly to the sound of trumpets ; but what attracted most attention, and what certainly had never been seen in our western armies, was a new kind of company, each soldier of which carried, instead of a shield, an immense kite, in the shape of a dragon. On the belly of the animal was fastened a placard, upon which a skilful pencil had traced, in huge red letters, verses that might have softened the princess's heart, supposing her to have understood Chinèse. It was labor lost ; they did not attract the least notice from the princess.

After the Chinese came a troop of barbarians ; a genuine horde of Attila. Dressed in wolf-skins, they resembled wolves, with their howls, gaunt forms, and savage gestures. At a signal from the chief they opened their ranks, to make way for a band of four hundred drummers, who instantly unchained the most formidable tempest of harmony that the world had ever heard. This was the serenade devised by a general as musical as he was gallant, to make a striking impression on the Fairest of the Fair. He succeeded beyond his hopes, for, at the first burst of thunder, the princess raised her hands to heaven, stopped her ears, and ran away.

V.

The crowd had vanished, night had fallen, and the moon shed her silver light on the tremulous waters of the lake, giving it by turns the whiteness and changing tints of the opal. Yielding to the neighing of his horse, that was tired of being alone, Prosper repaired to the inn. A fire of great logs was blazing in a huge chimney-place in which one might stand upright. Chilled by the night air, he drew near to warm himself, when he spied a strange object, looking like

" He was followed by a group of soldiers dressed in tiger-skins."

a bundle of rags that had been flung into the corner of the hearth.   As he gazed, from the bundle emerged a copper-colored face, round eyes with red eyelids, a nose hooked like a parrot's beak, a chin whose turned - up point seemed to

threaten the nose, and a toothless mouth that stretched from ear to ear.   The prince recoiled with dismay, when this shapeless mass rushed towards him, stretching out a pair of fleshless arms, and the witch—for witch it surely was—seized his hand and covered it with kisses.

"He spied a strange object, looking like a bundle of rags."

"My good lord," said she, in a plaintive voice, "do not drive me away. I am cold and hungry; if you have a mother, take pity on the wretchedest of women for her sake."

"Be easy, my good woman," answered the kind-hearted Prosper, touched by his mother's name. "You have nothing to fear from me. If you are suffering, I can at least relieve your want." And he opened his pouch, and flung a handful of gold into the lap of the witch, who clutched it greedily. "Yes," he added, "be happy, good dame. It is enough to have one unhappy creature in the house." His eyes filled with tears.

"My lord," said the old woman, rising, "you are sorrowful. What causes your sorrow—the Fairest of the Fair? You love her, you wish to carry her off, and you are in despair because you are unable to do so. It is the disease of the country. Tell me your troubles; I have friends everywhere; among the small and the great. Perhaps I can help you. She whom you have befriended is not ungrateful."

Prosper sat down by the table where his supper was laid, and told her his story. The old woman took a seat, without ceremony, opposite him, and listened with attention. "Very well," said she, when he had finished; "you are a good son, and it is a pleasure to be of use to you. Let me drink a drop, just one drop, of this Canary, to refresh my memory. It will give me ideas."

Upon which she seized the bottle, emptied it into a large goblet, and gulped it down at one draught, smacking her lips when she had finished.

"Confess," she said, "that all you suitors—Indian, Chinese, Tartar, and the rest—have very little imagination. There is but one way of entering the tower, and that is the only one you have never thought of."

"What is that?" asked the prince.

"Guess!" answered she; "and meanwhile, to refresh my poor memory, let me drink another drop, just a drop, of this Canary."

Upon which she seized another bottle, emptied it all into

the great goblet, and gulped it down at one draught, smacking her lips when she had finished. Then she turned towards the prince, who stood aghast at this conduct, and laughed in his face.

"Who has been in the tower? No one, you tell me. You are wrong. I see the swallows go in there every moment, and if the princess does not take care, she will have a whole garrison of crows on her hands."

"Do you think, then," exclaimed the prince, angrily, "that some crow will take me on its wings and fly up there, and then carry me off with my booty? You are making a laughing-stock of me, old dame."

"My lord," returned the witch, coldly, "people do not make a laughing-stock of princes before their faces. I am in earnest; I mean that you should go up there on horseback, as befits a noble personage like yourself."

"On horseback! My good woman, the Canary has sharpened your imagination altogether too much; you had better hold your tongue, and sleep it off."

"Yes, on horseback," continued the old woman. "Have you never heard of Pegasus, and of the hippogriff? Are you ignorant of history? And Bellerophon, and Perseus; have you forgotten them? Cannot you, too, deliver the new Andromeda?"

And, as the prince shook his head,

"Know," she said, "that ten leagues from here, in the stables of the Marquis of Lindas Piernas, is a flying horse named Griffon, that would make nothing of carrying you to the Fairest of the Fair. The whole secret is to know his language, and to make him fly. I will teach you his language if you will kiss me on both cheeks. As to making him fly, that is another matter; for this, you must have something which I have in my pocket, and which I will give you on the same terms."

She thrust her hand among her rags, and drew out a mass of chicken bones, frogs' legs, little wax figures, long needles, and finally a broken bit, held by two silken cords. "Here it is," said she; "the noble courser can only endure this light rein."

" And now," she added, simpering, " be good-natured, and give me a kiss."

The prince made a frightful grimace, which he tried to hide by biting his lips ; then, shutting his eyes, he kissed the old woman on both her cheeks, which were like parchment.

" One good turn deserves another," said the witch, and, approaching him, she blew into his mouth, and exclaimed :

" Nun kannst du die pferdische, eselische, burschikosiche, katzenjam-merische Sprache, sprechen und verstehen."

" A miracle !" cried the prince ; " I hear an ass braying in the yard, and this is what he says, '*Hi! han!* men are even more stupid than they are wicked. *Hi! han!*' An excellent thought, and well worthy of an ass!"

"Or of a philosopher. The two are well matched. And now, my dear prince, do you want the bridle?"

For his sole answer, Prosper clasped in his arms the old woman, who struggled against him. "Oh! these men!" she cried; "how beautiful they always think us when we do as they wish!"

But the prince did not listen; he was so happy that he kissed her frantically, with his eyes shut, and thought her cheeks as fresh as at twenty. He was not far from right, for on opening his eyes he saw before him, instead of the witch, a charming woman, whose smile disclosed teeth of dazzling whiteness. He attempted to thank her again, but she gently retreated. "That is enough," she said, "more would be showing too much gratitude. Adieu, prince; it is well to have a godmother who does not forget you. Have courage and hope!"

Like a gallant knight, the prince bent his knee to the ground; but as he laid his hand on his heart and was about to protest his eternal gratitude, the fairy disappeared, laughing in his face. It appears that there is no Academy in Fairy Land, and that no one ever speaks there when he has nothing to say.

VI.

At daybreak the next morning Prosper set out in search of the famous Griffon. On the way he learned that the Marquis of Lindas Piernas would allow no one to enter his stables. He disguised himself as a groom, and applied for employment to the chief equerry of the marquis. This personage, a fat, bow-legged, red-nosed man, dressed in the Spanish fashion, listened contemptuously, with both hands thrust in his girdle, and answered that raw louts were not wanted in the marquis's stables.

"Give me a horse," cried the prince, angrily, "and see if I do not know how to manage him better than all your bearded clowns."

For his sole answer the fat man turned his back on him. At this moment a groom came running up, out of breath, and, raising his hands to heaven, cried, "Oh! my lord, there is another accident, the tenth within a month! Joseph has had his leg broken by that fiend of a horse that no one can tame. He will be the death of all of us."

"Bah!" said the equerry, "you don't know what you are talking about. Here is a fellow from I know not where, who thinks he can teach you all. Give him Joseph's place, and put up another bed in the hospital."

Prosper followed the frightened groom. On entering the stable he saw a coal-black horse with a large head, full, prominent eye, powerful chest, and thin flanks, that stood drawn up, with arched neck, casting sidelong glances that boded no good.

"There is the famous Griffon," said the groom; "the wretch is plotting a kick for us or some new trick. Any one may go near him that will; I shall take care to keep out of his way."

The prince picked up a large whip and snapped it five or six times; then sang the following song at the top of his voice:

"He! juchhe! he juchhe! juch heisa! heisa he! he juchhe! juchhe! heisa he!
  Liebst du mich, ich liebe dich; Liebst du mich nicht, ich liebe dich nicht.
  Juvallera, juvallera, juvallevallera!"

Oh, power of harmony! At these melodious words, Griffon relaxed his neck, raised his head, and answered, in his language, by a prolonged neigh, of which Prosper did not lose a word :

" Kommen sie her, Schelm. . . ., und küssen sie mich Landsmann."

The prince did not wait to be bidden twice, but went straight to the horse and began to stroke him.

" Who are you," said Griffon, " and why have you come here ? Are you going to free me from the hands of these fools, who want to make a circus-horse of a grandson of Pegasus ?"

" Yes, my dear Griffon, I bring you your liberty ; but one good turn deserves another. Listen to what I expect you to do ;" and, as if he were afraid that some one might hear, he whispered his project in the horse's ear.

" All right," said Griffon ; " we will carry off the princess, but on one condition ; living or dead, you must always keep me with you. I have had enough of menageries."

" Done," answered the prince ; and he caressed Griffon.

While they talked together like old friends, all the stable-men gathered around in amazement ; and the equerry, who had been sent for, hastened to the spot.

" Well ! well ! young man," said he, " I see you and the horse are on excellent terms. Bring him out, and let us put him through his paces."

The prince took from his pocket the magic bridle. The horse once saddled, he sprang on his back, and rode upon a track where some race-horses were exercising. Every one looked at Griffon, who seemed clumsy, and hard to manage. Suddenly he quickened his pace and overtook the other horses, that, four abreast, filled the track ; then leaped over them with one bound. Thirty paces farther on he retraced his steps, leaped again over the heads of the coursers and

their astonished jockeys, and returned to the starting-point without having turned a hair.

"Prodigious!" exclaimed the equerry; "I never saw the like. I will bet that this beast could jump over the moon if he tried."

"Mr. Equerry," said the prince, gravely, "I take the bet."

And as all stood agape, he shouted two words in the horse language, which no one understood, whereupon Griffon drew

himself up, darted like an arrow through the air, and vanished from the eyes of the astonished crowd.

VII.

The clock had struck six. The Fairest of the Fair was
wearily promenading on the balcony of her prison, while below, in the valley, Indians, Chinamen, elephants, horses, and

drums were continuing their monotonous round. Suddenly,
she spied a black speck in the distance advancing rapidly
through the air. Was it a cloud, a gigantic bird, or some

strange monster? As it approached the tower the thing took shape, and the Fairest of the Fair clearly perceived a horse swimming in the air, and upon this horse a handsome rider, richly dressed, with embroidered tunic, velvet cap, and floating plume. Her first emotion was fear; and she thought of flight. Her second was curiosity—she was a woman and captive. Nothing, moreover, proved that the horse would stop in his mad course; but when it landed on the platform, and she saw Prosper alight and offer her his hand, she was so overcome with surprise that she swooned. The prince was ready to receive her in his arms, but he was terrified at her pallor and unconsciousness. "Griffon, my friend, she is dying," he cried. "We are lost! What is to be done?"

"Carry her off, my lord," answered Griffon, "carry her off;

we have no time to lose : you can settle matters on the road.
There is no better time for mutual explanations than when
a thing is done and cannot be undone."

Prince Prosper was so excited that he hardly knew what
he was about. He seated the princess on the horse, passed
his arm round her waist, and pressed her to his heart to keep
her from falling. As to Griffon, he gave a joyful neigh, and
darted into space like a bird spreading its wings to cleave
the air.

It was high time. A terrible crackling was heard. The
tower of glass broke into a thousand pieces, and melted

away in the lake, which instantly overflowed. Princes, elephants, horses, and drummers all fled pell-mell, and proba-
bly more than one of them was drowned. As to what be·
came of the Green Isles, no one ever knew. No trace of
them is found on the maps. The savans have formed nine
hundred and sixty-four hypotheses as to the discovery of
these lost lands, all of which are so probable that the subject
remains a perfect muddle to this day.

VIII.

One cannot remain forever in a swoon. By degrees the
princess regained her senses, but it took some time for her
to understand what was going on around her. Griffon soared
above the clouds, illumined by the last rays of the sun ; and
it seemed to the Fairest of the Fair as if she were passing
through a valley of snow, bordered with purple and gold
mountains. In attempting to move, she perceived that her
head was resting on Prosper's shoulder ; but she felt so
weak that she did not dream of raising it. All that she
could do was to ask the handsome cavalier who he was ; and
it was with a certain pleasure that she learned that he was
a prince, and that he tenderly loved his mother.

"And where are we going?" she asked, with a smile.

"To the palace of the King of the Bitter Waters."

"Is he your brother, kinsman, or friend ? Is he young
and handsome? What is the matter that you do not
answer?"

Prosper turned pale, and attempted in vain to open his
lips. Then, making a desperate effort to control himself, he
stammeringly told her of his mother, the wonderful bird, and
the pledge he had made. The princess suddenly sat upright, and pushed away the arm about her waist.

"Let me go," she cried, "I do not need your support.

What, was it for others that you tore me from my home and family, and that to exchange me for a parrot. We read of such things in fairy tales without believing them. What had I done to you to be treated in this way?"

"Alas," said Prosper, "I had never seen you when I made that rash promise."

"Ah! unhappy that I am," cried the princess, "behold me alone, delivered up to a barbarian, without a friend, and forsaken by all!" She sobbed, and shook convulsively with grief. The terrified prince once more supported her with his arm; she let him do so in silence, like one who knew not what she did.

This state of affairs could not be prolonged without peril, but happily Griffon went faster than the wind. At daybreak they were in the kingdom of the Bitter Waters. The king was celebrating his birthday by a grand review. They saw from above the troops drawn up on the plain. Loud shouts of "Long live the King" attested the love of the people for their prince. Griffon began his descent by circling in the air like an eagle that leaves his rock to swoop down into the plain, and landed before the king's palace with his double load in the most gallant fashion.

Prosper alone alighted from the horse. He saluted the king, and, speaking in a whisper that the Fairest of the Fair might not hear, told the story of his feats, and, in exchange for the princess, claimed the wonderful bird whose conquest had cost him so dear.

"Very well," said the king, who was eying Griffon rather than the princess, "I know what I promised; but first of all I must have that horse, otherwise the bargain is broken."

"That cannot be," answered Prosper; "you ordered me to bring you the Fairest of the Fair, and here she is.

It is your turn to keep your promise; a prince's word is
sacred."

"Do you dare to brave me?" cried the king. "Learn,
young man, that a king does what he pleases, and is bound
to no one. I shall keep the princess, the horse, and the
bird into the bargain. Begone this instant, and presume
no longer on my goodness!"

"Disloyal prince and false knight," exclaimed Prosper,

"you shall pay with your life for your breach of faith ; stand,
and defend yourself !"   Then, drawing his good sword, he fell
upon the King of the Bitter Waters, who had barely time to
put himself on guard.   The struggle was short ; the king
counted upon his magic to overcome Prosper ; but the
prince's sword was enchanted ; and at the very first en-

counter it pierced the throat of his foe, who threw up his
arms and fell motionless on the ground.   An instant after,
the corpse was nothing but a heap of dust and ashes, which,
as my readers all know, is the usual end of sorcerers.

The king dead, the palace doors opened of their own accord ; the enchantment was ended.   A host of princes, who

had resumed their own shapes, ranged themselves round their deliverer. At their head was Prince Lofty, followed by Prince Reckless, who bore the wonderful bird on his wrist, as a falconer carries his hawk. At this sight the troops disbanded ; all the generals and high officials clustered around Prosper, and offered him the crown, shouting " Long live the King !" The people and soldiers echoed the cry, and the rejoicing was universal.

Prosper thanked them all. His ambition was in a different direction ; but, in order not to disoblige them, he offered them in his place Prince Reckless, who was endowed from birth with all the qualities of a great sovereign. They were in need of a ruler, and had no time to wait ; moreover, Prince Reckless was very nearly as good-looking as his brother. The generals proclaimed him king ; the officers of the crown applauded ; the people and soldiers echoed the cry ; and the rejoicing was universal.

Meanwhile, Prosper approached Griffon, and, bowing to the Fairest of the Fair, who was still mute and pensive.

" And now, madam," said he, " where does it please you to be conducted by your faithful knight ?"

" Take me to your mother's house !" she answered, in a mournful tone, " I would not delay for a moment her pleasure in embracing so good a son."

IX.

People are right in saying that when Happiness enters a house Misfortune always stands on watch at the door to strangle it and take its place. Never had Prosper been so happy ; yet he was on the eve of losing everything, without even suspecting the danger by which he was threatened.

The coronation of Prince Reckless over, Prosper set out to rejoin his mother. The princess rode a snow-white nag,

which, by a strange instinct, clung close to Griffon's side ; a
fortunate circumstance, since Prosper and the Fairest of the
Fair constantly had some secret to confide to each other,
which could not have been of a tragic kind, since the pair
were always laughing.

. But behind them, with head bent, lips compressed, and
lowering brow, rode Prince Lofty, his heart consumed with
envy. "What," said he to himself, "must this boy return.
with the three wonders of the world, to be welcomed with
transport by my mother, the court, and my people, while I,
the eldest, come empty-handed, to be neglected by all. Am

I less brave or less generous than he? No, but luck was on his side and ill-luck on mine!" And he was beset by these evil thoughts, which he vainly tried to banish.

It chanced that on the third day they halted in a mountainous region, where there was a deep valley, at the bottom of which was heard a rushing torrent, while on the top of the cliff a narrow footpath followed the windings of the brook as it dashed among the rocks. The moon rose in all its beauty. Prosper went out to breathe the fresh air; he followed the footpath which led along the brow of the mountain, and admired the capricious play of the light and shade, thinking as he walked of all the dangers he had passed through, and of his happiness on seeing his mother again and presenting to her a daughter. His heart overflowed, and the toilsome past only rendered the present joy the sweeter.

But behind him, in the darkness, stalked an ungrateful brother and terrible foe. Hidden by the brush and rocks, Lofty had followed Prosper; why, he dared not own to himself. Hatred instinctively led him to dog the footsteps of his rival. Suddenly, a diabolical thought crossed his mind. Prosper was standing on the edge of the cliff, looking down at the brook as it glittered in the moonlight far down the valley. A false step, and he was lost. Lofty did not hesitate; he sprang upon his brother, and pushed him over the precipice. Prosper fell, uttering a cry; then nothing was heard but the noise of the stones as they rolled into the torrent and awakened the neighboring echoes.

The next morning, when the party was ready to go, Prosper was missing. Every one wished to wait for him, but Lofty harshly ordered them to proceed, and they were forced to obey. The prince was pale and haggard, and at the same time nervous and irritable. He attempted to mount Griffon and lead the way; but, in spite of a shower of abuse and

blows, the horse reared and kicked until he was left at liberty. He did not abuse it, but followed the princess with so meek and submissive an air that she took him in preference to her nag. The green bird also perched on the shoulder of its new mistress, and the train moved on without a word being spoken by any one.

After travelling four days in silence they reached the

kingdom of the old queen, who hastened to meet the procession, somewhat astonished at its gloomy air. It seemed more like a funeral train than a triumphal entry. On not seeing her dear Prosper, the poor mother burst into tears, which threw Lofty in such ill-humor that he left the party and shut himself up in his own apartments, and was not seen again until the next day.

A horse that does not neigh, a bird that does not sing, and a woman that does not talk are so far out of the common order of things that they can be accounted for only by magic. The good queen therefore affixed to the palace door a huge placard, offering an immense reward to any one who would make the lady speak and the bird sing. To keep off charlatans, however, a short shrift and a long rope were promised to all who proved by their failure that they were not sorcerers. It was the custom in olden times thus to treat those who promised marvels in order to build their fortunes on others' credulity. The custom had its advantages, and it is somewhat of a pity that it ever fell into disuse.

Half a dozen had already been hung, and the rest were beginning to be disheartened, when one day a new aspirant rang the great bell at the palace entrance. The unhappy man was brought into the main hall on the ground-floor, and warned of the fate there was in store for him. He did not seem dismayed, but shook his head in an ironical fashion. He was an old peasant, clad in goat-skins ; his shaggy white locks fell over his face, and he walked, leaning on a thick staff, with a slow but firm tread. He approached the throne where the queen was sitting, and was about to speak, when, lo ! the bird began to sing. "E desso," said he, in his jargon. At the same instant Griffon came on a gallop, and leaped the wall, neighing, "Da ist der Herr !" and, strange to say, the princess placed her hand on her heart and mur-

mured, "It is he!" All gazed at each other; when, quicker than lightning, the pretended peasant snatched off his wig, and threw himself into the queen's arms. It was Prosper, younger and handsomer than ever.

He turned to look for his brother; he was so happy that he was ready to forgive him. But Lofty had fled, and never more was seen; good luck, and good riddance to him! A wicked man the less in the world is a boon to all honest people.

How it happened that Prosper was still living; whether he had been caught by the brush on the rocks, or, what was more probable, whether his fairy godmother had caught him as he fell, and laid him in safety on the opposite bank, is something on which history is in doubt, and I do not venture to hold an opinion. It is certain, however, that the marriage of Prosper and the Fairest of the Fair took place without delay. The guests came from eight hundred leagues round, and Prince Reckless was there with all his court. It was a magnificent spectacle. In thirty days' feasting and dancing they spent the revenues of the whole year, and were forced to double the taxes.

But the people were highly amused; so much amused, indeed, that for years to come they dated everything from the marriage of Prince Prosper. Happy country, where the people can be amused at their own expense!

The festivities over, the bird proposed to the old queen to make her young again. "I shall be very glad," said she, "but do not go too far. At no price would I be willing to live over again the pleasures and vexations of youth. I should like to be a youthful grandmother, that I might see my grandchildren grow up ; I desire nothing more, and would not exchange my grandmother's crown for a bridal wreath." The bird did as it was told, and stopped when the old queen had gone back to the age of forty-five.

Prince Prosper and the Fairest of the Fair had a large family, and lived happily. Griffon stayed with his young masters, as did likewise the parrot, and they all grew old together. The bird more than once proposed to Prosper to make him young again, but he always refused. " No," said he ; " there are but three beings in the world that know how to love : an old dog, an old horse, and an old wife. I have found two of these treasures, and I mean to cling to them." On her side, the princess, woman though she was, refused to renew her youth. " What is the use," said she, " as long as my husband is satisfied with me as I am ? Whoever is beloved is always young and handsome."

Thus their lives were passed—loving, beloved, trusting, and happy. Their mutual affection was darkened by no cloud ; and, if they are not dead, they are loving each other to this very day.

THE FAIRY CRAWFISH.

AN ESTHONIAN TALE.

In the neighborhood of Revel, near the shores of the Baltic, there once lived a wood-cutter in a wretched hovel, situated by a deserted road, on the edge of the forest. Loppi, for that was our hero's name, was as poor as Job, and likewise as patient. That nothing might be lacking to complete the resemblance, Providence in its mercy had granted him a wife who might have given points to the spouse of the patriarch. Her name was Masicas, which signifies, it is said, wild strawberry. She was not naturally vicious, and never flew into a rage when other people agreed with her or did as she liked. But the rest of the time she was not so good-tempered. If she was silent from morning to night, when her husband was in the fields or the forest, she scolded from night to morning, when her lord was in the house. It is true that, according to the old proverb, "horses quarrel when there is no hay in the rack;" and plenty did not reign in the wood-cutter's hut. The spiders spun few webs there, for there was not a fly to catch, and two mice that chanced to stray into the wretched dwelling perished with hunger.

One day, when there was nothing to eat in the house, and the charming Masicas was more vixenish than usual, the honest wood-cutter flung over his shoulder an empty sack, his sole possession, and rushed from the house sighing. He used to go out with this wallet every morning in search of work, or, rather, of alms, too happy when he could carry home a crust of dry bread, a head of cabbage, or a few potatoes bestowed on him in charity.

He was passing by a pond, lighted by the first beams of day, when he spied in the wet grass a blackish object, lying motionless, and looking like some strange animal. It was a huge crawfish, whose like he had never seen. The morning sun, or perhaps fatigue, had put the creature to sleep. To seize it around the body and fling it into his sack, without giving it time to look about, was the work of an instant. "What a windfall!" thought Loppi; "and how pleased my wife will be! It is long since she had such a treat."

He leaped with joy; then suddenly stopped and turned pale. From the sack arose sepulchral tones—a human voice; it was the crawfish speaking.

"Halloa! my friend," it cried, "stop, and let me go. I am the oldest of the crawfish tribe; I am more than a hundred years old. What could you do with my tough carcass? It would blunt the teeth of a wolf. Do not abuse the chance that has thrown me into your hands. Remember that I, like yourself, am one of God's creatures, and pity me as you would some day have him take pity on you."

"My dear crawfish," answered the wood-cutter, "your

"The honest wood-cutter flung over his shoulder an empty sack, and went out sighing."

preaching is fine, but do not blame me for not listening to your sermon. For my own part, I would willingly let you go, but my wife is waiting for me to bring her our dinner. If I return empty-handed, and tell her that I caught the finest crawfish that ever was seen, and let it go again, she will raise an uproar that might be heard from here to Revel. And, with her quick temper, she is quite capable of meeting me with a broomstick."

"What need is there of telling your wife?" asked the crawfish.

Loppi scratched his ear and then his head, and, heaving a deep sigh,

"My dear," said he, "if you knew Masicas, and understood how sharp she is, you would not talk to me in this style. She has a way of leading you by the nose, whether you will or no. There is no resisting her. She turns you inside out like the skin of an eel, and makes you tell all you know, and even some things that you do not know. She is a superior woman."

"My dear friend," resumed the crawfish, "I see that you belong to the brotherhood of good husbands. I congratulate you! But as empty compliment will not serve your turn, I am ready to redeem my liberty at a price that will satisfy madame. Do not judge me by appearances. I am a fairy, and have some power. If you listen to me, you will be the gainer; if you turn a deaf ear, you will repent it all your life."

"Oh, dear," said Loppi, "I do not want to harm anybody. Fix matters so that Masicas will be pleased, and I am quite ready to let you go free."

"What kind of fish does your wife like best?"

"I have no idea. We poor people have not time to pick and choose. It is enough that I do not go home empty-handed. No one will complain."

"'Taking the crawfish around the body, he gently placed her in the water."

"Lay me on the ground," said the crawfish, "then dip your open sack into this corner of the pond. Right. Now, *Fish in the sack!*"

Was such a marvel ever seen! In an instant the sack was full of fish; so full, indeed, that it nearly slipped from its owner's hands.

"You see that she whom you have befriended is not ungrateful," said the crawfish to the astonished wood-cutter. "You can come here every morning and fill your wallet by repeating the words *Fish in the sack*. I will keep my promise. You have been kind to me, and I will be kind to you. And if, by and by, you wish for something else, come here and call me, in these solemn words,

> 'Crawfish, dear friend,
> Succor pray lend.'

I will answer your voice, and see what I can do. A last piece of friendly counsel: if you wish to be happy at home, be prudent; and say nothing to your wife of what has happened to-day."

"I will try, Madame Fairy," answered the wood-cutter. Then, taking the crawfish around the body, he gently placed her in the water, into which she plunged out of sight.

As to the proud and happy Loppi, he returned home with a light step and a lighter heart. He hardly waited to enter the house before opening his sack, when, behold, there sprang from it a superb pike, an ell long, a great golden carp, that leaped in the air and fell back gasping, two fine tenches, and a mass of whitefish. Any one would have said that it was the pick of the Revel market. At the sight of all this wealth Masicas uttered a cry of joy, and threw herself on Loppi's neck.

'My husband, my dear husband, my love of a husband,"

she said, "you see how right your little wife was in making
you go out so early this morning to seek your fortune. Another time you will listen to her. What splendid fish! Go
to the garden, where you will find a little garlic and onions,

then run to the woods and get some mushrooms. I will make you a fish soup such as king nor emperor ever tasted. Then we will broil the carp ; and we shall have a feast fit for an alderman."

The meal was a merry one. Masicas had no will but that of her husband. Loppi thought that the honeymoon had come again. But, alas! the very next day, which was Monday, the fish he brought were more coldly received. On the fourth day madame made a face at them, and on Sunday she burst forth in a passion.

" Have you vowed to shut me up in a convent ? Am I a nun, that you condemn me to keep Lent to all eternity ? What can be more insipid than this fish ? The very sight of it turns my stomach."

" What do you want, then ?" cried honest Loppi, who had not yet forgotten his destitution.

" Nothing but what every honest peasant family has to eat. A good soup, and a piece of roast pork ; that is all I need to be happy. I am content with so little."

" It is true," thought the wood-cutter, " that the fish from the pond is a little tasteless, and that there is nothing so good for a weak stomach as a nice slice of pork. But will the fairy be able to grant me so great a favor ?"

The next morning, at daybreak, he hastened to the pond and called his benefactress :

> "Crawfish, dear friend,
> Succor pray lend."

And behold, a huge claw rose from the water, then another, and then a head in a bishop's mitre, with two great staring eyes.

" What do you want, brother ?" asked a well-known voice.

" Nothing for myself," answered the wood-cutter. " What

have I to wish for? But my wife has a weak stomach, and
is beginning to tire of fish; she would like something else;
soup, for example, or a roast of pork."

"If that is all your dear wife needs to make her happy, I
can satisfy her," answered the crawfish. "At dinner-time
tap thrice on the table with your little finger, saying **each**

time, '*Soup and roast appear!*' and you will be served.   But
beware : your wife's wishes may not always be so modest ;
do not become a slave to them, or you will repent when it is
too late."

"I will try," said Loppi, sighing.

At the appointed hour the dinner appeared on the table.
Masicas was overcome with joy.   The gentleness of a lamb
and the tenderness of a dove were nothing compared with
the submission she showed her husband.   These halcyon
days lasted a whole week.   But ere long the horizon darkened, and at last the storm broke on the head of the innocent Loppi.

"How long is this torture to last ?   Do you mean to sick-
en me to death by feeding me on this greasy broth and fat
pork ?   I am not a woman to stand such treatment."

"What do you want then, my love ?" asked Loppi.

"I want a good, plain dinner : a roast goose, and some
tarts for dessert."

What answer could he make? There were a number of things, indeed, that he might have said, but Loppi was not equal to risking the peace of the family. A look from his wife would have made him sink into the earth. One is so weak when he loves!

The poor man did not close his eyes that night. Early the next morning he set out for the pond, and walked for a long time up and down the bank, his heart consumed by anxiety. If the fairy thought he was asking too much, what was he to do? At last he summoned up his courage, and cried,

> "Crawfish, dear friend,
> Succor pray lend."

"What do you want, brother?" answered a voice that made him start.

"Nothing for myself. What have I to wish for? But my wife's stomach is beginning to tire of soup and roast pork. She would like something light; for instance, a roast goose and some tarts."

"Is that all?" replied the good fairy, "we will try once more to satisfy her. Return home, brother, and do not come to me every time your wife wishes to change her bill of fare; let her order what she likes; the table is a faithful servant, and will obey her."

No sooner said than done. On returning home, the woodcutter found the table already laid, with pewter mugs and plates, wrought-iron spoons, and three-pronged steel forks; the fairy had done things on a grand scale, to say nothing of the roast goose and potatoes, stewed sauce, and toothsome plum-pudding. Nothing was lacking, not even a flask of anisette cordial to enliven the feast. This time Loppi thought his troubles at an end.

Alas! it is sometimes a misfortune for a husband to in-

spire his wife with too high an idea of his might.   Masicas had sense enough to understand that there was something magical about this wonderful plenty.   One day she insisted on knowing what good genius had taken them under
his protection.   Loppi attempted at first to keep silence, but
how could one resist so trusting, tender, and loving a wife?
Let the first husband that would not do likewise dare to
cast a stone at him and tell it at home; I shall think him
rasher than Alexander, and bolder than Cæsar.

Masicas had sworn to betray this precious confidence to

no one ; she kept her oath (there was not a neighbor within two leagues around) ; but if she kept the secret, she took care not to forget it.

An occasion soon offers to him who is on the watch for it. One evening, when Masicas had delighted her husband with her tenderness and good-humor, " Loppi," she said, " my dear Loppi, you have been lucky, it is true, but you do not know how to make the most of your luck. You do not think about your little wife. I dine like a princess, and dress like a beggar. Am I so old and ugly that you are willing to let me go ragged? I do not say this through coquetry, my love ; there is but one man whom I care to please ; but I must have clothes like a lady. Do not tell me that you cannot help it," added she, with the most winning smile, " I know better ; I know that the fairy is always ready to serve you. Can you deny the modest request of her who lives for you alone?"

When a woman asks for a dress to shine only in her husband's eyes, who could be barbarous enough to refuse to please his companion, even though it took a new toilette every day. Loppi was not a monster. Indeed, in the bottom of his heart, he thought that Masicas was not wrong. With their squalid garments, it seemed as though they were eating stolen food. How much brighter their table would be with a well-dressed mistress of the house at its head !

Despite these good reasons Loppi set out for the pond in an uneasy frame of mind. He began to fear that he was going too far. It was not without dread that he called his benefactress—

> " Crawfish, dear friend,
> Succor pray lend."

Suddenly the fairy appeared above the water. " What do you want, brother ?" said she.

"Nothing for myself. What have I to wish for? But you are so good and generous that my wife's wishes come a little too fast. Her rags remind her of our former wretchedness, and nothing will do but that she must be dressed like a lady."

The good crawfish laughed heartily. "Return home, brother," said she, "your wife's wishes are granted."

Loppi could not find words to express his thanks, and insisted on kissing the claw of his friend. He sang along the road, as gay and light-hearted as a lark. On the way he met a beautiful lady, dressed in cloth, silk, and furs. He bowed humbly to the noble princess, when the stranger laughed in his face and flung herself on his neck. It was Masicas, in all her beauty, and, to speak frankly, she was second to none in majesty and grace. The proverb that the habit makes the monk and the feathers the bird, is, above all, true where women are concerned.

This time Masicas was happy, there was no denying it; but it is the misfortune of the happy that desires beget desires. Of what use was it to play the lady when she lived alone in a wretched hovel, without a neighbor to madden with jealousy at her sight, or a mirror in which to gaze at herself from head to foot? Masicas had not promenaded about in her cloth and furs for a week when she said to her husband,

"I have been thinking about the way we live; it is really absurd. I will stand it no longer. A princely table and elegant dress do not agree with a hovel open on all sides. The fairy has too much sense, and she loves you too well, my dear husband, not to feel that she owes us a mansion where I can play lady of the castle all day long. With this, I shall have nothing left to desire."

"Alas! we are lost," cried Loppi. "The string that is

drawn too tight is sure to snap; we shall be poorer than ever. Why not be content with what we have? How many would be thankful for such comfort as ours!"

"Loppi," said Masicas, impatiently, "you will never be

anything but a milksop. Don't you know that those who are afraid to speak for themselves always go to the wall? Are you any the worse for taking my advice? Go on; don't be afraid; I will answer for the consequences."

She railed at the good man until he set out, his limbs trembling beneath him. Should the fairy refuse to listen, he could bear the disappointment well enough, but how could he face his wife's despair on his return? He did not feel able to brave the tempest she would raise; and the only way in which he could summon up his courage was to vow within his heart that if the crawfish said no, he would fling himself head foremost into the pond. However violent might be the remedy, the evil was still greater.

Nothing is braver than poltroons at bay. It was in a gruff voice that he cried:

> "Crawfish, dear friend,
> Succor pray lend."

"What do you want, brother?" said the fairy.

"Nothing for myself. What have I to wish for? But my wife, in spite of all the favors you have heaped upon us, torments me night and day to make a new demand of you, against my will."

"Ho, ho!" cried the crawfish, "you have changed your tune. You have told our secret to your wife; now you may bid farewell to peace at home. And what does this fair lady ask, now that she thinks she has me in her power?"

"A mansion, good fairy, a modest little castle, that her house may correspond with the fine clothes you have given her. Make Masicas a baroness, and she will be so happy that we shall have nothing left to wish for."

"Brother," answered the crawfish, gravely, "be it as your wife desires." And she abruptly disappeared.

Loppi had some trouble in finding his way back. The whole aspect of the country had changed; around him were well-tilled fields, and pastures full of cattle; beyond he saw a brick mansion, in the midst of a garden full of fruit and flowers. Wondering what this castle could be, which he beheld for the first time, he gazed at it with admiration, when a richly dressed lady came down the steps. Strange to say, she smiled at him and held out her hand—it was Masicas.

"At last," she exclaimed, "I have nothing left to wish for. Kiss me, my dear Loppi. You have crowned my wishes. I thank you, and also the good fairy."

The honest wood-cutter was ravished with delight. No dream could have been more enchanting. In an hour to be transported from poverty to riches, and from obscurity to a lofty station; to dwell in a castle with a graceful woman, always good-humored, and whose only thought was to please him—Loppi wept for joy.

But, unhappily, there is no dream without a waking. Masicas tasted all the pleasures of wealth and greatness. All the barons and baronesses in the neighborhood disputed with each other the honor of visiting and receiving her; the governor of the province was at her feet; and her dresses, castle, horses, and stables were the talk of the whole neighborhood. Had she not the finest trotters in the country; English cows with scarcely any horns and still less milk; English hens that seldom laid, but that were as handsome and wild as pheasants; and English pigs so fat that neither head, tail, nor feet could be seen? What did Masicas lack, then, to make her the happiest of women? Alas, everything had succeeded but too well with her. She felt that she was born to rule, and did not hide it from her husband. The great lady wished to be a queen.

"Do you not see," said she to Loppi, "with what respect every one treats me? It is because I am always in the right. Even you, who are more stubborn than a mule, cannot help owning that I am never wrong. I was born to be a queen! I feel it."

Loppi cried out in amazement. He was sharply told in reply that he was nothing but a simpleton. Who had forced him, against his will, to apply again to the crawfish? It would be the same way this time. He would be king, in

" A richly dressed lady came down the steps."

3*

spite of himself, and it was to his wife that he would owe his crown.

Loppi had no wish to reign. He breakfasted well and dined

better ; his desires went no further. But he loved his repose before everything, and he could not be ignorant that, with his beloved better half, he could enjoy repose only on condition of submitting to madame's will and caprices. He scratched his head and sighed ; it is even said that he swore a little ; but he set out, and on reaching the pond called in a tender voice to his dear friend the crawfish.

He saw the black claws rise from the water, and heard the "What do you want, brother?" but stood for some time without speaking, himself appalled by the temerity of his request. At last he answered,

"Nothing for myself. What have I to wish for? But my wife is beginning to be tired of being a baroness."

"What does she want, then?" asked the fairy.

"Alas!" murmured Loppi, "she wants to be a queen."

"Ho, ho!" cried the crawfish. "It was a lucky thing for her and you that you saved my life; this time also I will grant your wife's wish. Hail, husband of a queen, I wish you much joy! Good-evening, Prince Consort!"

When Loppi returned home the castle had become a palace; Masicas was a queen. Valets, chamberlains, and pages were rushing about in all directions to execute the commands of their sovereign.

"God be praised," said the wood-cutter, "I have found rest at last! Masicas is at the top of the ladder; she can climb no higher; and she has so many around her to do her will that I can sleep in peace without her insisting on waking me."

Nothing is more fragile than the happiness of kings, unless it be that of queens. Two months had hardly passed when Masicas had a new whim. She sent for Loppi.

"I am tired of being queen," she said; "I am sick to death of the platitudes of these courtiers. I wish to rule over free men. Go for a last time to the fairy, and make her give me what I desire."

"Good heavens!" cried Loppi, "if a crown does not satisfy you, what will? Perhaps you would like to be God himself?"

"Why not?" answered Masicas, coolly. "Would the world be any the worse governed?"

On hearing this blasphemy, Loppi gazed at his wife.

" The castle had become a palace ; Masicas was a queen."

aghast. The poor woman had evidently lost her mind. He shrugged his shoulders.

"Say and do what you like," said he, "I shall not trouble the fairy with such folly."

"We will see about that," cried the queen, in a rage. "Do you forget who I am? Obey me instantly, or off goes your head."

"I will go as fast as I can," cried the wood-cutter. "I may as well die one way as another," thought he; "as well by the hand of the fairy as that of my wife. Perhaps the crawfish will have pity on me."

He staggered like a drunken man, and found himself on the edge of the pond without knowing how he came there. He cried at once, in despairing accents,

> "Crawfish, dear friend,
> Succor pray lend."

There was no answer. The pond remained silent; not even the buzz of a fly was heard. He called a second time; there was no echo. Terrified, he called a third time.

"What do you want?" said a harsh voice.

"Nothing for myself. What have I to wish for? But the queen, my wife, makes me come here for the last time."

"What more does she want?"

Loppi fell on his knees.

"Forgive me, it is not my fault! She wants to be God."

The crawfish rose half-way out of the water, and, stretching a threatening claw towards Loppi, cried,

"Your wife deserves to be shut up in prison, and you to be hung, wicked fool. It is the cowardice of husbands that causes the folly of wives. To your kennel, wretch, to your kennel!"

And she dived into the pond in such a rage that the water hissed as if a red-hot iron had been dipped in it.

Loppi fell face downward upon the ground as if struck by lightning. When he set out for home, with hanging head, he knew but too well the road he had travelled so often ; the edge of the forest, bordered with puny birches and sickly firs, stagnant pools here and there, and, farther on, a wretched hovel ; he had relapsed into direr want than ever.

What would Masicas say, and how should he comfort her ? He had not much time for these melancholy thoughts ; for a hag, in tatters, flung herself on his neck as if to strangle him.

" Here you are at last, you monster !" cried she. " It is you that have ruined us by your stupidity and folly. It is you that have enraged your accursed crawfish. I might

have expected it. You never loved me; you never did anything for me; you have always been a selfish wretch. Die
by my hand!"

She would have torn out his eyes, if he had not with great
difficulty held both her arms.

"Take care, Masicas, be quiet; you will hurt yourself."

It was lost labor; Loppi felt himself giving way, when
suddenly the veins in the throat of the fury swelled, her face
turned purple, she threw herself back, flung up her arms, and
fell heavily on the ground. She was dead; rage had killed
her.

Loppi mourned for his wife, as every good husband ought to do. He buried her with his own hands under a great fir-tree in the neighborhood. Over the grave he placed a stone, and surrounded the whole with a rough wall to keep off the wild beasts of the forest. This sad duty fulfilled, he returned home and strove to forget.

But he fell a prey to despair; he was not made to live alone. "What shall I do; what will become of me?" he cried, weeping. "Here I am, solitary, forsaken, a burden to myself. Who will think for me, choose for me, speak for me, and act for me, as my dear wife used to do? Who will waken me a dozen times in the night to tell me what I must do to-morrow? I am nothing but a body without a soul, a corpse. My life fled with my beloved Masicas. I have nothing left but to die."

He spoke truly. Early the next winter, a peasant on his way through the forest saw a man lying in the snow. It was Loppi, who had been dead a week—dead of cold, hunger, and sorrow, without a friend or neighbor to close his eyes. His icy fingers grasped an awl, with which he had traced on the stone this last tribute to her who had been the delight of his life—

TO THE

BEST OF WIVES,

FROM THE

MOST INCONSOLABLE OF HUSBANDS.

FRAGOLETTE.

I.

In the neighborhood of Mantua there once lived an orphan, already a tall girl, who went to school every morning with her books and dinner-basket. The school was not far off, but it took a long time to go there, for the way led along a ditch, lined with bushes and great trees, full of blossoms, fruit, birds, and butterflies, according to the season. Who could help stopping to look at all these wonders of creation?

One day our school-girl spied in the heart of a wild rose the prettiest blue butterfly that ever was seen. She held her breath, as she advanced on tiptoe, and gently raised her hand, when the butterfly slipped through her fingers, fluttered to the right and left, and settled a little higher up the slope. She followed, it flew away, alighted on a flower

farther up, and flitted thus from place to place, until it led her up the side of the ditch, near a walled enclosure, which bore a bad reputation in the neighborhood. This was the spot, it was said, where the fairies danced in a ring on Midsummer Eve, and witches held their Sabbaths on dark winter nights. Although the walls had crumbled in many places, and filled up the ditch, no Christian dared venture into this accursed place ; but butterflies have no scruples, and children are like butterflies.

Our blue-winged traveller unceremoniously entered this garden, which looked like a virgin forest, and the little girl followed, carried away by the pleasure of the chase. But scarcely had she pushed through a clump of bushes when she stopped short and cried out with wonder. Before her was a meadow, bordered with large trees, and dotted with red and black spots which enamelled the turf. They were great, luscious strawberries, strawberries that had no owner, and that offered themselves to any one ready to profit by this wasted treasure. Forgetting the butterfly, the school-girl threw herself on her knees in the grass, and, in less than a quarter of an hour, filled her basket; after which she took to her heels, and arrived at the school out of breath, and with cheeks redder than the strawberries she had gathered. She was scolded for coming so late; but she was so proud and happy that she did not hear a word that was said to her. What is the use of laying down the law to con-querors!

At luncheon-time she divided her treasure with her little friends, who could not sufficiently praise her courage and good luck. She seemed like a queen surrounded by a host of courtiers. Nothing was wanting to her triumph. They called her Fragolette, which means in French, Little Straw-

berry, and this title she kept all her life. At least, it is the only name by which she is known in history.

It is true that there were timid souls who could not rid themselves of certain scruples. While eating the strawberries, they questioned whether it might not be tempting the devil to rob him on his own ground ; but these idle murmurs were lost in the tumult of victory ; and no one paid any attention to them.

It would have been better to have listened to them, as the sequel of our story proves. Intoxicated with her good fortune and popularity, Fragolette returned again and again to the spot, and finally began to look upon the place as her own. " It is a deserted field," she thought, " whose fruit is devoured by the blackbirds and thrushes ; and surely a Christian has quite as much right to it as the birds."

One day, however, when she was gathering her harvest, as usual, a frightful blow on the head stretched her on the ground. " I have caught you, you thief," cried a terrible voice, " you shall pay for this !"

Stunned by the blow, Fragolette tried to rise, when she saw before her a figure, the very sight of whom froze her with horror. It was a tall, thin, yellow, wrinkled old woman, with red eyes, and a nose like the beak of a vulture. From her gory mouth projected two teeth, longer and sharper than a wild boar's tusks. Fragolette tried to stammer an apology ; but the old woman, who was a witch, and an ogress into the bargain, did not deign to hear a word ; she tied her hands behind her, wound a rope seven times round her waist, and made a running knot in it, through which she passed the handle of the enormous broom with which she had knocked down the child.

Then, muttering in the devil's language some of those horrible words which make the earth tremble and the

"When she was gathering her harvest, as usual, a frightful blow on the head stretched her on the ground."

heavens turn pale, she seated herself astride the broomstick, and darted like an arrow through the air, carrying with her the unhappy Fragolette, suspended in space, like a spider hanging from its web.

If she had ever studied geography she might have enjoyed the magnificent spectacle spread out beneath her, of beautiful Italy, bordered by the snowy Alps and the blue ocean, and traversed by the verdant ridges of the Apennines ; but in those days women spun on their distaffs at home, and troubled themselves little about what was taking place in China and Peru—geography was of small use to them ; and, besides, the poor child was too frightened to open her eyes. She passed over Vesuvius and Etna without seeing them, and was more dead than alive when the magic broomstick descended to the earth amid the forests of Sicily.

"Up, little brigand," said the witch, pulling her by the hair, "you belong to me now ; begin your work. Go, set the table in the dining-room. How I should like to eat you if you were not so thin !" she added, feeling her arms ; "but in my house people soon grow fat, and you will lose nothing by waiting." With this horrible jest, she opened wide her great mouth, and licked her lips with a smile that made poor Fragolette shudder.

The dinner was not very merry, as may be thought. The old woman greedily devoured a roast of cat, mice in jelly, and stewed turnips. Fragolette gnawed a crust of bread, and threw herself, in tears, on a wretched pallet that was laid for her in a corner. Happily, she was of the age when slumber is stronger than sorrow, and she had scarcely touched the ground when she fell asleep.

II.

The day after this sad adventure Fragolette's slavery

began. Every morning she was forced to sweep and dust the whole house, cook the meals, set the table, wash the dishes, and, what was worst, help to dress her frightful mistress. She stood for whole hours curling the only three hairs that the ogress had on her head, after which she had to clean her two great teeth, and put rice-powder, rouge, and court-plaster patches on her face; and she was lucky, indeed, when all this painting was done, if she was let off with three or four boxes on the ear

Nevertheless, in spite of this hard life, Fragolette grew taller and prettier every day. I do not say that she grew better, for she was not one of those good creatures that stoop to kiss the hand that strikes them ; no, indeed, her blood boiled in her veins, and she dreamed only of rage and vengeance. The old hag saw this—people always fear those whom they injure. Often, while Fragolette was curling her hair, she wondered whether her servant might not seize the opportunity to throttle her, and whether it would not be wise to be beforehand with the girl.

One day, when Fragolette seemed to her more beautiful than ever, she was seized with anger and jealousy.

"Take this basket," said she to the young girl, "go to the fountain, and bring it back full of water; if you do not, I will eat you up."

The innocent girl ran at full speed, fancying that the basket was enchanted, and that the witch was amusing herself by frightening her, as usual. She dipped the basket into the fountain, but, on lifting it up, the water all ran out, as from a sieve. Three times she tried to fill it, and three times her labor was in vain. At last she understood that the ogress meant to kill her. Filled with rage and despair, she leaned against the fountain and burst into tears. Suddenly she heard a gentle voice saying, "Fragolette, Fragolette, why do you weep?" She raised her head, and saw a handsome young man looking at her tenderly.

"Who are you," she said, "and how do you know my name?"

"I am the witch's son, and my name is Belebon. I know that she has resolved to take your life, but she shall not succeed, I promise you. Give me a kiss and I will fill **your** basket."

"Kiss the son of the witch! Never!" said Fragolette, proudly.

"Well, I will be less cruel than you," answered the young man. And, breathing three times on the basket, he dipped it into the fountain and drew it out full of water. Not a drop escaped.

Fragolette returned to the house, and set the basket on the table without saying a word. The ogress turned pale as death.

"Do you, by chance, belong to the trade?" said she, staring the young girl full in the face. Then, striking her forehead, she said, "You have seen Belebon, and he has helped you; own it."

"You must know, since you are a witch."

For her sole answer the hag dealt her such a box on the ear that she had to cling to the table to keep from falling.

"Ho, ho!" cried the witch, "we shall see who will win! He laughs best who laughs last!"

The next day the ogress said to Fragolette, "I am going to take a trip to Africa. I shall be back this evening. You see that sack of wheat; it must all be made into bread before I return. It is no harder than to carry water in a basket. If you do not succeed, look out for yourself!"

Saying this, she went out chuckling, and locked the door.

"This time I am lost," cried the young girl. "How can I grind the grain, and knead and bake the bread? I have neither mill nor oven, nor time to do it." She beat upon the door again and again, hoping to break it open and escape. It was opened by Belebon.

"Fragolette, Fragolette," said he, "I only wish to do you good; give me a kiss, and I will make the bread and save you."

"Kiss the son of the witch!" answered Fragolette, trembling. "Never!"

"You are pitiless, Fragolette, but I cannot let you die."

He whistled, and, behold, from all the holes in the house came a host of rats and mice. The rats carried the wheat to the mill, and came running back with a sack of flour; after which, they heated the oven while the mice made the bread. And when the witch returned it was all baked; and the golden loaves were piled to the ceiling.

"Wretch!" cried the old woman, "you have seen Belebon, and he has helped you; own it."

"You must know, since you are a witch."

The ogress dealt her a savage blow, but Fragolette suddenly stooped, and her enemy fell forward, striking her nose on the table, and turned blue with rage and pain.

"Ho, ho!" cried she, "we shall see who will win! He laughs best who laughs last!"

III.

Three days later, the hag, putting on her most smiling countenance, called Fragolette. " My child," said she, " go to my sister's house, ask her for her casket, and bring it to me."

" How am I to know where your sister lives, or what she is called ?"

" Nothing is easier," answered the witch ; " go straight forward till you come to a torrent that crosses the road, ford it, and a little farther on you will see an old castle, with an iron gate, where my sister, Viperine, lives. Go, and hurry back, my child."

" What a miracle !" thought Fragolette; " the old witch is in good-humor."

Saying this, she set out with a light step. On the way she met Belebon, who was waiting for her.

" Where are you going this morning ?" he asked.

" I am going to my mistress's sister, to fetch back her casket."

" Unhappy girl !" cried Belebon, " you are sent to your death. No one ever quitted Viperine's castle alive. But I can save you. Give me a kiss, and I will answer for your safety,"

" No, I will never kiss the son of a witch !"

" Fragolette, Fragolette, you are ungrateful ; but I love you better than my life, and will save you in spite of yourself. Mark me well ; when you have reached the brink of the torrent, you must say, ' Beautiful river, let me pass through thy silvery waters !' Then take this bottle of oil, loaf of bread, rope, and small broom. On reaching the iron gate of the old castle, rub the hinges with oil and it will open of its own accord. A great dog will spring at you, barking ; throw him this bread and he will stop. In the courtyard you will see

a poor woman drawing water from the well by tying the
bucket to her braids of hair; offer her this rope; go up the
steps and you will find in the kitchen another woman clean-
ing the oven with her tongue, give her this broom. Then go
into the chamber where Viperine is asleep; the casket is on
a cabinet, seize it, and escape as fast as you can. If you
obey me you will not die."

"The gate, rubbed with oil, opened of its own accord."

Fragolette forgot nothing that Belebon had told her. On the brink of the torrent, she cried, "Beautiful river, let me pass through thy silvery waters!" and the nymph of the torrent answered in her sweetest tones, "Pass, lovely girl," whereupon the waters parted so that she passed over dry-shod. The gate, rubbed with oil, opened of its own accord. The dog pounced on the bread, turned round, curled

himself up, and lay down, his head on his paws, looking lovingly at Fragolette. The two women joyfully took the gifts that were brought them, and our heroine noiselessly entered the room where Viperine lay snoring. She ran to the cabinet and seized the casket. Her heart beat loudly, and she thought herself saved, when suddenly the witch awoke. Fragolette was already on the steps.

"Ho! ho! there!" cried Viperine; "woman in the kitchen, kill that thief for me!"

"Not I," answered the victim; "she has given me a broom, while you make me clean the oven with my tongue."

"Woman at the well," cried the witch, "seize that thief and drown her!"

"Not I," answered the victim; "she has given me a rope, while you make me draw up the bucket with my hair."

"Dog, tear her to pieces!"

"Not I," said the mastiff, without even raising his head; "she has given me bread, while you let me die of hunger."

"Door, shut her in!"

"Not I," said the door; "she has oiled my hinges, while you let me be eaten with rust."

The witch reached the bottom of the steps with one bound; but the door, delighted at regaining its liberty, swung back and forth without ceasing, and, just as Viperine was about to go out, it closed upon her so suddenly that she was nearly crushed by it.

Fragolette ran on without looking behind her, but, in her terror, she did not forget to pay a compliment to the river, and passed over as before. Viperine was close behind her. "You dirty brook," said she, "open a way for me or I will dry you up!"

The torrent parted; but when Viperine was half-way over the waters suddenly rose, and closed upon the witch, who was instantly drowned. The nymph had avenged herself.

On reaching home, Fragolette gave the casket to her terrible mistress. What a figure the ogress cut can well be imagined. "This is a new trick of Belebon's," she thought, "but I know another worth two of that. He laughs best who laughs last!"

IV.

That night she made Fragolette sleep in her room. "Mark me well," said she, "in the poultry-yard there are three cocks, one red, one black, and the third white. To-night, when one of these cocks crows, you must tell me which it is. Look out for yourself if you guess wrong; I will make but one mouthful of you."

"Belebon will not be here," thought Fragolette; "I am lost," and she did not close her eyes for an instant.

At midnight a cock crew.

"Which cock was it that crowed?" asked the witch.

"Belebon," whispered Fragolette, "tell me which it was."

"Give me a kiss," murmured a voice, "and I will tell you."

"No."

"Cruel girl, I will not let you die ; it was the red one."

The witch sprang from her bed and approached Fragolette.

"Answer, or I will eat you up."

"It was the red cock that crowed," said Fragolette, trembling.

And the witch went back to bed, grumbling.

At the same instant, another cock was heard.

"Which cock was it that crowed?" asked the witch.

And Belebon whispered the answer to his beloved,

"It was the black one."

And the witch went back to bed, grumbling.

At daybreak, the cock crew again.

"Belebon, help me," cried Fragolette.

"Give me a kiss," said he; "I have borne your cruelty long enough."

And behold, the witch came near, opening wide her gory mouth.

"Belebon, Belebon," cried the child, "if you forsake me, it is you that will be my murderer!"

"It was the white cock," answered Belebon, unable to resist her tenderness.

"It was the white cock," cried Fragolette.

"No matter, traitress," exclaimed the ogress, in a rage, "your time is come; you must die."

With these words she fell upon her prey.

But Fragolette, young and agile, slipped from her hands, opened the window, and leaped into the garden. The furious witch prepared to follow her, but her foot caught in the window, she fell head foremost, and broke off both her teeth— those teeth on which her power and life depended. Beneath the window lay a corpse!

V.

Left alone with Belebon, Fragolette soon began to wonder what would become of her. To return to her own country scarcely crossed her mind; she was an orphan, and all there had forgotten her. To stay in the house where she had suffered so much was also out of the question. For his part Belebon said nothing; he was happy at having Fragolette near him, and dared not think of the future.

There came a time, however, when Fragolette claimed her liberty. Belebon dared not refuse to let her go; but he reminded the ungrateful girl of all he had done for her, and offered her his heart and hand.

"No," said Fragolette, "I will not marry the son of a witch."

"Go, then," said poor Belebon, "go, since nothing will keep you. But before leaving this house, where I shall die without

you, give me at least one token of friendship—the only one I shall have ever received from you. Put your hand in mine and forgive me the crime of my birth. We will not part as strangers."

She gave him her hand, which he took and covered with kisses; she did not withdraw it, and looked at him in a strange fashion.

"Farewell," said Belebon, "you take with you my happiness and life. Blessed, a hundred fold blessed, be him to whom you give this hand."

"Since you have it, you may as well keep it," said she.

He fell on her neck, sobbing; and she, the capricious girl, took his head in her hands, and kissed his forehead, laughing and crying at the same time. No one can ever tell what is passing in the heart of a woman. Two days after, they were married.

Thus ends the story; but it is natural to ask what became of the pair. Did Belebon continue his mother's wicked practices? Did Fragolette and her husband return to the life of common mortals? I wrote, on this subject, to a learned Sicilian, a member of the Academies of Catania, Agrigentum, and other places, and this is his answer :

"Most illustrious and reverend seignior :—

"I have been unable to find in our ancient chronicles the name of either Fragolette or Belebon. Distrusting my own humble erudition, I have consulted very learned brethren of all the Academies, and their answer has been that among all the peoples who successively conquered Sicily—Pelasgians, Sicanians, Phœnicians, Greeks, Carthaginians, Romans, Arabs, Normans, Spaniards, and others—there never had been seen a married man who was a wizard. We have reason, therefore, to believe, by analogy, that Belebon, once married, was no worse than the rest."

Such is the opinion for which I asked, and it seems to me wise and just. I refer the point to my readers, both male and female, and especially to the latter.

THE THREE WISHES.

There was once a wise emperor who made the following law: Every stranger who comes to court shall be served with a fried fish. The attendants shall carefully watch the new-comer; and if, after eating the fish down to the bone, he turns it over to eat the other side also, the man guilty of this unheard-of crime shall be instantly arrested, and hung three days after. But, through our imperial grace, the culprit may each day make a wish, which shall immediately be granted, provided he does not ask for his life.

There had already been more than one victim to this legal caprice, when one day a count, followed by his young son, appeared at court. The two noble guests were welcomed in the warmest manner; and, in accordance with the law of the emperor, a fried fish was served up to them in the midst of their repast. Both father and son relished it heartily; and,

after eating down to the bone, the count turned over the fatal fish. He was instantly seized by two attendants and dragged before the emperor, who ordered him to be thrown into prison. This filled the young son of the count with such grief that he begged the emperor to let him die in his father's stead. As the emperor was not cruel, and, provided some one was hung, cared little who it was, he accepted the exchange, shut up the son in prison, and let the father go free.

Once in his dungeon, the youth said to his jailers, "You know that, before dying, I am entitled to three wishes. Go

to the emperor, and tell him to send me his daughter and a priest to marry us directly."

A man more astonished than the emperor at this insolent demand it would be hard to find. But a sovereign's word is sacred, and he can hardly break his own law. His daughter, moreover, was resigned to this three days' marriage; and, like a good father, the emperor gave his consent.

The next day the prisoner asked the emperor to send him his treasure. This demand was little less audacious than that of the day before; but what can be refused a man who is to be hung on the morrow? The emperor, therefore, sent him his money and jewels, which he immediately proceeded to divide among all the courtiers; and as at that time there chanced to be those at court who were weak enough to be fond of money, they began to take an interest in this poor young man who had been so well brought up.

On the third day, the emperor, who had slept badly, went himself to the culprit. "Come," said he, "make haste to tell me your last wish, which, once granted, you shall be strung up without delay, for I am beginning to be a little tired of your unreasonable demands."

"Sire," said the youth, "I have but one more favor to entreat of your majesty, after which I shall die contented. It is to put out the eyes of all those who saw my father turn over the fish."

"Very well," answered the emperor. "Your demand is quite natural, and does credit to your goodness of heart."

Upon which he arrested the major-domo.

"I, sire!" cried the major-domo; "I saw nothing of the kind; it was the cupbearer."

"Seize the cupbearer," cried the emperor, "and put out his eyes."

But the cupbearer declared, with tears, that he had seen nothing; he referred to the taster, who referred to the butler, who referred to the pantler, who referred to the first waiter, who referred to the second, who referred to the third; in short, no one had seen the count turn over the fish.

"Father," said the princess, "I appeal to you as a second Solomon. If no one saw it, the count is not guilty, and my husband is innocent."

The emperor frowned, and the court at once began to murmur; he smiled, and every mouth grinned from ear to ear.

"All right," said he; "let this handsome innocent live. I have hung more than one who was no more guilty than he. But if he is not hung, he is married; justice is done."

THE GOLDEN FLEECE.

A SERVIAN FAIRY TALE.

I LOVE the Servians; they are a brave people, who remind me of the heroes of Homer. Their war-songs are epics, and their fairy tales have the freshness and grace of the marvellous stories of the East. As a specimen, here is one of the most celebrated, which an aged spinster on the banks of the Morava lately related to Vouk Stephanovitch.

At Kroujevatz there was once a hunter by the name of Ianko Lazarevitch. He was the king of the mountain. Though his only worldly wealth was a little cottage surrounded by an orchard, he lived there in peace and plenty, with his wife and child. His bees supplied him with honey, his plum-trees furnished him the best brandy in the country, and, thanks to his carbine, game was never lacking on his table. The rich have their fields, mines, and treasures ; Ianko had his forest. The hares, roes, and bucks, for ten miles round, belonged to him ; and when fine fox-skins or superb bear-furs were wanted at Belgrade, Widna, Pesth, or even Con-stantinople, to whom did men go for them but to Ianko, the hunter of Kroujevatz ?

Happiness is like the flower of the fields ; it withers in a day. On a fine winter's night, as Ianko was lying in wait for game, he spied a strange light in the distance. The for-est-trees were lighted up for an instant as if by a passing torch, then fell again into shadow, while the light went on. At the same time he heard a heavy tread and the sound of crackling boughs. Ianko instantly quitted his hiding-place, and ran to see what was the matter, when there rushed from the forest a huge ram, whose eyes darted fire, and whose fleece glittered like the sun. He raised his carbine, but the beast sprang upon him quicker than lightning, and hurled him to the ground.

The next morning at daybreak some wood-cutters, on their way to work, found the poor hunter stretched on the earth, and already cold in death. Two deep wounds were in his breast, from which his life-blood had ebbed. The wood-cutters carried the body of their brave comrade back to town ; he was buried, and all was over. In the happy dwelling, which had so often rung with Ianko's merry songs, nought was heard but the wails of a widow and the sobs of a child.

Joyous or sad, the years pass away, bearing with them our pleasures and sorrows. Stoian, the son of Ianko, grew up to manhood, and his chief desire was to be a hunter. His father's blood flowed in his veins, and, while still a child, it had been his greatest delight to look at and handle the car-bine hanging on the wall. But, when he asked his mother

to give him the fatal weapon and let him go to the forest,
the poor woman burst into tears.

"No, my child," she said, "nothing will induce me to -
give you that carbine. I have already lost my husband
through it, and must I also lose my son?" Stoian held his
peace, and kissed his mother, but the very next morning he

renewed his entreaties, and was so tender and caressing, and promised to be so prudent, that she finally yielded.

Early in the morning Stoian hastened to the mountain, intoxicated with joy. He hunted all day long, and at night took up his watch at the very spot where his father was killed.

The night was dark, and the tired young hunter was falling asleep in spite of himself, when he was aroused by a loud noise. He perceived a strange light; he saw the forest-trees lighted up one after another, as if by a torch, and heard a heavy tread and the sound of crackling boughs. Without quitting his hiding-place, Stoian raised his carbine and commended himself to God. Suddenly there rushed from the forest a huge ram, whose eyes darted fire, and whose fleece glittered like the sun.

"Stoian! Stoian!" he cried, "I killed your father, and have come to kill you!"

"No," answered the young man; "with God's help, it is I who will kill you."

He took aim so truly that the bullet struck the ram between the eyes. He sprang in the air and fell as if struck by lightning.

Stoian threw himself on the beast, and was beginning to skin it, when suddenly there appeared at his side a tall woman with raven tresses and green eyes. It was the Vila, or fairy of the mountain.

"Stoian," said she, "you have delivered me from an enemy; take my hand; I am your sister. When you are in need of help, call on me."

The young hunter thanked the lady, and went down the mountain to Kroujevatz, happy, and proud of his game. The fleece of the ram was hung on the wall, where it lighted up the whole cottage. The entire province came to admire

it, and Stoian was proclaimed king of the mountain, like his father. There was not a young girl that did not smile on him as he passed by.

In those days the Turk (whom God confound!) was master of Servia. Raschid, the pacha of Belgrade, was an old janizary, who, perhaps, had been brave in his time, but who was now nothing but a coarse and selfish old man, who spent his life in drinking, smoking, and sleeping. To aid in ruling a people whose language, religion, and customs he despised, he kept near him a renegade from none knew where—one of those miscreants, without faith or law, who live only by plunder. Yacoub, for that was the name of this honest man, had a low forehead, eyes like a weasel's, a nose as hooked as the beak of an eagle, and ten fingers, even crookeder than his nose. Of all the words in the language, the one he knew best was the verb *take*, and this he conjugated in all its moods and tenses. As to the verb *restore*, he was ignorant of it. May Satan teach it to him to all eternity!

It is a common saying that one Turk makes more havoc than half a score of wolves, and that, in this respect, one renegade is equal to half a score of Turks. Yacoub did not belie the proverb. One day, when Raschid had come to Kroujevatz to hunt, Yacoub, according to custom, set about collecting the taxes on his own behalf. It is just to say, however, that he gave something to his master, who gave nothing to the sultan.

On entering the house of Stoian the renegade was dazzled by the golden fleece. His eyes sparkled and his hands clenched with envy.

"My son," said he to the young hunter, "that is a beautiful specimen. The pacha ought to know all the animals of his forests; carry him that fleece. It belongs to him."

"The fleece is mine," answered Stoian, "and I shall not give it away."

"Who talks of giving?" returned the renegade; "with the great men of earth every gift is a barter. The pacha, my master and yours, is too generous to remain under obligations to a raya."

"I do not sell my property; I keep it," replied Stoian.

"Weigh your words, young man," said Yacoub, with a frown. "Pride goeth before a fall, and the pacha's arm is long. I want this fleece, and must have it."

For his only answer Stoian took down his carbine, and showed the renegade the door.

"Don't be rash, my son," said Yacoub, hurrying out; "you may some day regret not taking my advice."

On his return to the palace, the renegade found Raschid

gulping down glass after glass of the white wine of Semen-
dria.

"Taste this wine," said he to Yacoub ; "it is tokay.   If
the cadis were to try it, they would give their whole Koran
in exchange for a bottle."

"The vintage is excellent," answered the renegade, "but

it is not as good as the white wine I drank at Smyrna. It is true that the pacha there has a vine which bears grapes without their equal."

"He is very fortunate," said Raschid, drinking deeper and deeper every moment.

"What hinders you from being as fortunate as he?" continued Yacoub. "There is in this country a certain Stoian, a kind of sorcerer, who could plant you such a vine, and make it bear grapes in a week. But perhaps he might raise some difficulties about it."

"Difficulties!" exclaimed the Turk, shrugging his shoulders. "Send a janizary, and tell him that if, within a week, I have not a vine as fine and grapes as good as those of Smyrna, I will cut off his head."

"That is an argument that admits of no reply," said Yacoub, laughing heartily. He added to himself, "The golden fleece is mine."

On receiving this terrible message, Stoian burst into tears. "Alas! mother, we are lost!" he exclaimed.

"My son," said the poor woman, "did not I tell you that the carbine would cost your life, as it did your father's?"

In despair, the young man rushed from the house, and wandered onward, not knowing whither he went. On reaching the mountain he met a young girl, who said,

"Brother, why do you weep?"

"God be with you!" answered Stoian, roughly; "you cannot help me in my trouble."

"How do you know?" rejoined she; "it is by trying them that we learn what our friends are worth."

The hunter raised his head, and recognized the Vila. He threw himself, weeping, into her arms, and told her of the wickedness of Yacoub and the folly of the pacha."

"Is that all?" said the fairy. "Courage, brother! I am

here. Go to the pacha, ask him where he would like to have his vine planted, and tell him to have the trenches dug. Then take a sprig of basil, plant it in the trench, and sleep peacefully in the new garden. Before a week is past you will gather ripe grapes."

Stoian did as the Vila had bidden him. On the first day he planted the sprig of basil ; but he had little confidence in the fairy's promises, and went to sleep with a heavy heart. He rose before daybreak, and ran to the spot ; the shoots were already above the ground. The second day they grew tall ; on the third they put forth leaves ; on the fourth they blossomed. On the sixth day the grapes were golden, although it was only spring - time. Stoian gathered and pressed them, and carried to his terrible master a jug of new wine and a plate of ripe grapes.

At the sight of this wonderful vintage, every one was astonished except the pacha, who thought it quite natural, and did not even thank poor Stoian. Nothing is easier, says the proverb, than to catch snakes with other people's hands.

"Well," said Raschid to Yacoub, "what do you think of my power? I am not a sorcerer, and I am proud of it. He who wields the sword needs neither wealth nor knowledge ; the purse and brains of others all belong to him."

"I marvel at your highness's genius," answered the renegade, bowing low, "and hope that you will not leave your work unfinished."

"Is anything lacking to my vineyard?" asked Raschid, with a dissatisfied air.

"It lacks the ivory tower which, at Smyrna, is the admiration of the faithful and the despair of unbelievers."

"Is that all?" said the pacha, laughing. "Come here, young man. If, in a month, I have not an ivory tower like that of Smyrna, I will cut off your head. Hear and obey!"

Stoian ran to his mother, weeping. "Alas, we are lost!" he cried.

"Go, my son, hasten to the mountains; perhaps you will find there our friend and protectress."

The young man hurried to the mountain, and called the fairy three times. She came, smiling, and listened to him with tenderness.

"Is that all?" she said. "Courage, brother! I am here. Go to the pacha, and ask him for a ship, three hundred tuns of wine, two hundred pipes of brandy, and a dozen carpenters. Set sail and steer straight ahead. When the vessel is between two mountains, go on shore, empty the pond that you will see there, and fill it with wine and brandy. When the elephants come thither at night to quench their thirst, they will drink until they fall dead-drunk. Let the carpenters saw off their tusks, and you will have a full

cargo of ivory. Then return to the vineyard with your booty, take with you a sprig of basil, and sleep tranquilly in this new garden ; in a week the tower will be built."

Stoian did all that the Vila had bidden him. The vessel anchored between two mountains ; they emptied the pond, and filled it with wine and brandy. At nightfall the elephants came thither in herds. The first that tasted the brandy seemed astonished; but he soon went back to it with delight, and the rest followed his example. A scene of jollity, noise, and general confusion followed. The whole elephant nation kept holiday. In contempt of etiquette, the king of the elephants danced a hornpipe, and the queen waltzed with a young chamberlain. The whole company soon fell sound asleep, and the carpenters began their work. Do not blush at this humiliation, good people of Elephant Land; you are not the first nation that have had their teeth filed while drunk or asleep, and you will not be the last.

On his return, Stoian had the huge mass of ivory piled in the garden. From his hiding-place behind the wall Yacoub watched the young hunter, in hopes to steal his secret; but Stoian spent the whole day in singing plaintive songs, accompanying himself on the guzla. When night cast its veil over the earth, nothing was done. Yacoub went away rubbing his hands. "He is lost!" he thought; "the golden fleece is mine."

But the next morning the foundations of the ivory tower were laid; the day after it had risen to the second story; and on the sixth day it was finished, with its dome and minarets. For ten leagues round it shone in the sunlight with a brilliancy more dazzling than that of the silver moonbeams upon the waters.

At the sight of this marvellous structure all were astonished except the pacha, who thought it quite natural, and did not even thank poor Stoian.

"Well," said he to Yacoub, stroking the handle of his ataghan, "what do you think of my power?"

"I marvel at your highness's genius," answered the renegade, bowing low, "and hope that you will not leave your work unfinished."

"Is anything lacking to my ivory tower?" asked Raschid, with a dissatisfied air.

"It lacks the Princess of the Indies. Of what use is the ivory tower if it does not contain the masterpiece of creation?"

"You are right," said the pacha. "It is the bird that gives value to the cage. Come hither, young man," said he to Stoian. "Go, fetch me the Princess of the Indies. If you return without this miracle of beauty, I will cut off your head. Hear and obey!"

Stoian ran to his mother, weeping.

"Alas! we are lost," he cried. "You will never see your child again."

"Go, my son, hasten to the mountain; perhaps you will find there our friend and protectress."

The young man hurried to the mountain, and called the fairy three times. She came, smiling, and listened to him with tenderness.

"Is that all?" said she. "Courage, brother! I am here. Go to the pacha, and ask him for a large ship. In this ship build twelve fine shops, and fill them with rarer stuffs and jewels than are to be found in all the bazaars of Constantinople. In these shops put twelve of the handsomest youths of Servia, dressed like princes. Then set sail, and when the ship stops between two mountains, go on shore; you will be in the kingdom of the Indies. Take your guzla, sing with your companions, and when the girls of the country come to the fountain, invite them to see the treasures in your ship. Make them presents; they will be delighted with your generosity, and, on returning home, will say that never was there seen a finer ship, richer treasures, or more obliging merchants. Being a woman and a princess, the daughter of the King of the Indies has a double share of cu-

riosity. She will come to see you : amuse her all day, but
as soon as night falls, weigh anchor and set sail. But when
the princess is on board, the task is not done. She is a magician, and may put you more than once in danger. Follow
my counsels, however, and you will succeed."

Saying this, the fairy drew near the brook that trickled
down the mountain, and called a salmon that was swimming
up the stream. She detached a scale from it, which she
gave to Stoian.

"Take this talisman," said she. "If ever you need a service done you in the depth of the sea, throw this scale into
the water, and call my brother, the salmon, to your aid."

Then, raising her eyes to the sky, the Vila saw a falcon
chasing a dove. She whistled, and both birds flew to her,
and perched on her shoulder. She pulled a feather from
the falcon's crest, and another from the wing of the dove,
and gave them to Stoian.

"Take these talismans," said she ; "and if ever you need a
service done you in the air, fling these feathers on the breeze,
and call to your aid my brother, the falcon, and my sister,
the dove. And now farewell, brother. I have exhausted for
you all the secrets of my art ; you will see me no more."

Stoian thanked his sister, the Vila, and did all that she
had bidden him. The vessel stopped between two mountains ; the young girls came to the fountain, they listened to
the songs of Stoian, they came on board, they took the
choicest gifts without much urging, and that very evening
they repeated throughout the town, "Never was there seen
a finer ship, richer treasures, or more obliging merchants."

The next morning the Princess of the Indies, followed
by twelve companions, came to the shore in a magnificent
howdah, borne by the gentlest and handsomest of elephants. She carried on her shoulder a little parrot, that

" The Princess of the Indies, followed by twelve companions, came to the shore."

diverted her with its chatter. Stoian hastened to meet the lady, and did her the honors of his ship. At each shop the richest stuffs were spread before her, and the rarest jewels, rings, bracelets, necklaces, and diadems displayed before her eyes. The princess and her attendants were as fascinated as larks before a mirror ; and the day passed without their being able to tear their astonished and delighted gaze from such wonders.

As soon as night fell upon the sea Stoian weighed anchor and set sail. At the first motion of the ship the princess took alarm: she hastened on deck, and, taking the parrot on her finger, " Fly, dear bird," she said, "and tell my father some one is carrying off his child."

The parrot took flight, but Stoian instantly flung on the breeze the falcon's feather, and cried, " Brother Falcon, come to my aid !"

And, lo ! a black speck was seen far off on the horizon ; the falcon darted through the air, pounced upon the parrot, and carried it to a rock to devour it.

The princess looked at Stoian with a disdainful air, and threw her ring into the sea, when, lo ! the ship instantly stopped as if it were aground. It was in vain that the wind filled the sails—a hidden power held the vessel motionless.

Stoian flung into the waves the scale of the salmon, crying, " Brother Salmon, come to my aid."

He had not done speaking when the rich scales of a huge salmon were seen shining through the water ; then the fish dived and caught the ring, upon which the vessel floated swiftly over the sea, impelled by the fairest of winds.

The princess cried out, and hastened below to her companions. At daybreak the next morning she came again on deck, and said to Stoian,

" With a word I could turn this ship to stone, and you

would never more see your country. But if you will give me the water of immortality, I am ready to go with you. Do you see yonder rock, where a thick smoke is rising? There is a fountain, guarded by two dragons, whose nostrils breathe fire. No one has ever been able to overcome the vigilance of those monsters, who sleep neither night nor day. If you can succeed where all others have failed, and can fill this little flask, I will be your most devoted friend and servant."

For his only answer Stoian seized the flask, and, flinging on the breeze the feather of the dove, cried,

"Sister Dove, come to my aid!"

In an instant a dove, white as snow, perched on Stoian's shoulder; she seized the flask in her beak, soared high in the heavens, and vanished from sight. In an hour she came flying back, and Stoian could offer the princess the water of immortality.

"Thank you, my friend," said she, in the tenderest of tones. "Now you have nothing more to fear from my power. Say, whither are you taking me?"

"To my master, the pacha," answered Stoian.

"Ah!" exclaimed she; and, drawing her veil over her face, she went below, and did not speak again to Stoian for the rest of the voyage.

When it was learned that the young hunter had returned, there was universal rejoicing at Kroujevatz. The people flocked from all directions to see the entry of the Princess of the Indies. It was a wonderful spectacle. First came the twelve attendants, each mounted upon a black horse, which was led by the bridle by one of Stoian's companions. Nothing more magnificent had ever been seen than these young men, with their rich garments, girdles glittering with gems, sabres with silver scabbards, and inlaid carbines. But all were forgotten at the sight of Stoian and his conquest. En-

veloped though she was in a long veil, which hid all but her
great black eyes, the princess eclipsed her companions as
the moon eclipses the stars. Her white horse seemed proud
to carry her. All the men admired her as she passed, but
the women looked at Stoian. Handsome, haughty, and melancholy, he attracted the gaze of all.

On entering the palace where the pacha was awaiting her
the princess threw aside her veil. At the sight of this marvellous beauty, Raschid, forgetting his age, hastened to her
with a tottering step, and attempted to embrace her. But
she repulsed him so roughly that, if the faithful Yacoub had
not been at hand, the pacha would have bruised his nose on
the ground, in spite of all his power.

"Ha! beautiful savage," cried he, "what has your faithful
slave done to be treated in this way?"

"You are an ill-bred fellow," answered the princess.
"You ask neither my name nor that of my father; you
know neither who I am nor what I wish. Am I a dog or a
hawk, to be taken thus by force? Learn that he who mar-
ries me must possess a twofold youth, that of the soul and
that of the body."

"I have a very youthful soul," said the pacha. "As to
the body, I should ask nothing better than to renew its age,
were it only to marry you, and live long by your side. But
how is it to be done?"

"I have found the means," returned the princess. "This
flask contains the water of immortality. Let yourself be beheaded! once dead, I will sprinkle you with this magic water, and will make you as young and handsome as at twenty."

The pacha made a grimace; then, looking round him, he
saw Stoian, and frowned.

"I believe in this marvellous water," said he; "but I
should not object to see it tried. What if I test it on this

"Handsome, haughty, and melancholy, he attracted the gaze of all."

fellow, whose looks I dislike, I know not why? Come here, raya; to make you young again, we will cut off your head."

"I am young enough to dispense with such a trial," answered Stoian, looking at the beautiful East-Indian; "but, though I perish, I will not shrink from danger. What matters life to me?"

At a sign from the pacha a janizary drew his sword, and with one blow struck off the young man's head. Every one uttered a cry of horror; but the princess instantly sprinkled the quivering body with her marvellous water; when, lo! Stoian rose full of life and health, and so young and handsome that the pacha, wild with jealousy, exclaimed,

"Make me young again, princess! Quick, without losing an instant!"

He called the janizary and gave him his orders; then, seeing Yacoub, who pretended to weep,

"Poor Yacoub," he said; "my faithful friend and right hand, I cannot let you remain old while I am young; we should no longer understand each other's wants. No, my friend, I am not selfish; I need you, and we must both renew our youth together. We will be beheaded at the same time."

At this mark of friendship Yacoub turned pale as death. He opened his lips and tried to speak, but the signal was given, and at the same instant his head rolled on the ground by the side of that of the pacha.

"Take away that carrion," said the princess, coldly, "and throw to the dogs the body of the wretch who dared treat me with insult."

At these words all looked at each other; the Turks frowned, but the Servians drew their sabres, and said, "The princess is right: an insult recoils on him who dealt it. Woe to him who does not respect a woman."

" The people flocked from all directions to see the entrance of the Prin
cess of the Indies."

An old Turk responded, "What is done is done. No one can escape his fate."

Peace restored, the princess said to Stoian, "Here I am, a widow without being married, and you are left without a master. Are you not going to take me back to my father?"

"No," cried Stoian; "the dearest right of a Servian is to carry off his wife, and I have twelve companions ready to follow my example."

"Stoian," said the princess, smiling, "you know that I dislike violence. What need is there of carrying me off? Will it not suffice to take me to your mother's house, and give me a place at your fireside?"

No sooner said than done, and the same day saw thirteen weddings at Kroujevatz.

Raschid had more than one successor, and there was more than one Yacoub; for wherever there is a pacha like Raschid, there is also a flatterer and a traitor; but the wicked profit by experience, and fear holds them in check. No one disturbed Stoian, and all respected the Princess of the Indies. The house is still seen where the pair dwelt, and strangers are shown above the door a stone, carved, it is said, by Stoian's own hands. On it are a carbine and yataghan, crossed; the whole surmounted by the motto, which is the delight of Servia and the terror of the Osmanli, *Svobodnost*, LIBERTY.

POOR HANS.

OLD Hans lay dying. His pastor sat by his bedside, offering the last consolations.

"Alas!" said old Hans, "life is small loss to me. ●I have never been anything but a poor wretch, bowed down with toil and pain. Where no one else wanted to go, there poor Hans was sent; and when others overturned the cart, it was Hans that had to set it up again."

"Rejoice then, my friend," said the pastor, "your sufferings will soon be over. Blessed are they who suffer, for theirs is the kingdom of heaven."

"Ah!" cried old Hans, "I am sure beforehand that it will be just the same up there. Every one will shout after me,

" Hans, light up the sun !"   " Hans, put out the moon !"

' Hans, light up the sun!' ' Hans, put out the moon!' ' Hans, let fly the thunder!' ' Hans, put the angels to bed!' "

And without even heaving a sigh, poor Hans closed his eyes, folded his hands, and breathed his last.

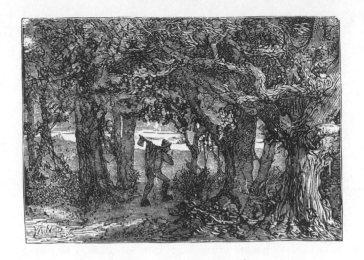

ZERBINO THE SAVAGE.

A NEAPOLITAN FAIRY TALE.

I.

ONCE upon a time there lived in Salerno a young wood-cutter named Zerbino. Poor and an orphan, he had no friends; shy and taciturn, he spoke to nobody and nobody spoke to him. As he never meddled with other people's business, every one took him for a fool. He was nicknamed The Savage, and never was title better deserved. In the morning, when the whole town was still asleep, he went to the mountain, with his jacket and axe on his shoulder; stayed all day in the woods, and did not return until dusk, dragging after him a bundle of fagots with which he bought his supper. When he passed the fountain where the young girls of the neighborhood congregated every evening to fill their pitchers and empty their throats, they all laughed at his glum face, and made a butt of the poor wood-cutter. Neither the black beard nor glittering eyes of Zerbino dismayed the bold huzzies, who vied with each other in jeering at the simpleton.

"Zerbino of my soul," cried one, "speak but one word to me and I will give you my heart."

"Delight of my eyes," exclaimed another, "let me hear the sound of your voice and I am yours."

"Zerbino! Zerbino!" cried all the madcaps in chorus, "which of us will you take for a wife? Is it I? Is it I? Which one will you have?"

"The greatest chatterbox of you all," answered Zerbino, shaking his fist at them; upon which they cried, "Thank you, good Zerbino, thank you!"

Pursued by shouts of laughter, the poor savage retreated home, with the grace of the wild boar fleeing before the hunter. His door once shut, he supped on a crust of bread and glass of water, rolled himself in a ragged old coverlet, lay on the bare earth, and instantly fell into a dreamless slumber, free from care and sorrow. If happiness consists in feeling nothing, Zerbino was the happiest of men.

II.

One day, when he had tired himself with hacking at an old box-tree as hard as flint, Zerbino thought he would take a nap by the side of a pool surrounded with spreading trees. To his great surprise, he found stretched on the turf there a lady of marvellous beauty, arrayed in a robe of swan's-down. The stranger seemed to be in a nightmare; with drawn features and clenched hands, she was vainly struggling to shake off a hideous dream.

"What folly to go to sleep at noon with the sun shining on one's face!" said Zerbino. "Women are all fools."

He wove some branches together so as to shade her head, and threw his jacket over the rude arbor.

6

Just as he had finished arranging the leaves he spied a viper in the grass, close by the stranger, that was crawling towards her and darting out its venomous tongue.

"What!" said Zerbino, "so small and yet so wicked!" And with two strokes of his axe he cut the serpent into three pieces, which writhed as if still trying to reach the lady. Zerbino kicked them into the pool, where they fell hissing like a red-hot iron dipped in water.

At this moment the fairy awoke and sprang up, her eyes sparkling with joy.

"Zerbino! Zerbino!" she shouted.

"That is my name; I know it; you need not scream so loud."

"What, my friend," said the fairy, "will you not let me thank you for the service you have done me? You have saved me from worse than death."

"I have saved you from nothing at all," answered Zerbino,

with his usual grace. "Another time don't go to sleep on the grass without looking to see whether there are any serpents about, that is my advice to you. Now good-day! Let me sleep; I have no time to waste."

He stretched himself his full length on the grass and closed his eyes.

"Zerbino," said the fairy, "have you nothing to ask of me."

"I ask you to let me alone. When a man wants nothing, he has all he wants; when he has all he wants, he is happy. Good-day!"

And the churl began to snore.

"Poor boy!" said the fairy, "your soul is asleep; but, say what you may, I will not be ungrateful. Had it not been for you, I should have fallen into the hands of a genie, my cruel foe; had it not been for you, I should have been turned into a viper for a hundred years. I owe you a hundred years of youth and beauty. How shall I pay you? I have it," she cried; "he who has what he wants is happy, you said yourself just now. Well, my good Zerbino, whatever you may desire, whatever you wish for, shall be yours. I hope you will soon have cause to bless the fairy of the waters."

She made three circles in the air with her hazel wand, then stepped into the lake so lightly that the waters were not even rippled. At the approach of their queen the reeds bowed their heads; the water-lilies opened their freshest blossoms; the trees, the sunshine, and the winds themselves all smiled on the fairy, and all seemed to share in her happiness. A last time she raised her wand, and the waters opened instantly with a flash of light, as if a sunbeam had pierced their depths, to receive their young sovereign. Then shadow and silence fell over all, and nothing was heard but Zerbino still snoring.

"She made three circles in the air with her hazel wand."

III.

The sun was beginning to decline when the wood-cutter awoke. He returned tranquilly to his task, and with a vigorous arm attacked the trunk of the tree whose branches he had lopped off in the morning. The resounding blows of the axe made no impression on the hard wood. Bathed in perspiration, Zerbino vainly smote the gnarled trunk, which defied all his efforts.

"Ah!" said he, looking at the jagged edge of his axe, "what a pity that some one would not invent a tool that would cut wood like butter. I should like to have one of that sort."

He drew back a step, whirled the axe around his head, and struck with such force that he fell flat, ten paces forward, with his arms outstretched, and his face on the ground.

"Pshaw!" he exclaimed, "I must see double; I struck on one side."

Zerbino was quickly reassured, for at the same instant the tree fell so near him that the poor fellow just escaped being crushed by it.

"That was a fine stroke," said he, "it helps my day's work amazingly. What a clean cut I made; it looks as if it were sawed. There is not another wood-cutter in the town that could have done it."

Upon this he gathered up all the branches that he had hewed off that morning, unwound a rope from his waist, seated himself astride the bundle of fagots, the better to tie them together, and fastened them with a slip-knot.

"Now!" said he, "I must drag them home. What a pity that bundles of fagots had not four legs like horses, so that I could gallop proudly into Salerno like a fine gentleman that rides about doing nothing. How I should like to see myself prancing into town in that fashion !"

And, behold, instantly the bundle of fagots rose and began to trot at a measured pace. Without being at all astonished, the honest Zerbino let himself be carried

along by this new kind of steed, and pitied the poor wretches on the way, who went on foot for want of a bundle of
fagots.

IV.

At the time of which we are speaking there was a great
square in the centre of Salerno, where the king's palace stood.
This king, as every one knows, was the famous Mouchamiel,
whose name is immortal in history.

Every afternoon the king's daughter, the Princess Leila,
might have been seen seated in her balcony in a melancholy
mood. It was in vain that her slaves attempted to amuse
her by their songs, tales, or flatteries—Leila listened only to
her thoughts. For three years the king her father had
sought to marry her to every baron in the neighborhood, and
for three years the princess had refused all suitors. Salerno
was her dowry, and she knew that it was her dowry alone

that they wished to marry. Earnest and tender, Leila had no ambition; she was not a coquette; she did not laugh merely to show her teeth; she knew how to listen, and never talked when she had nothing to say—a malady so rare among women that it drove the doctors to despair.

Leila was even more dreamy than usual, when suddenly Zerbino appeared on the square, guiding his bundle of fagots with the majesty of a plumed Cæsar. At the sight, the princess's two waiting-women were seized with a mad fit of laughter, and, happening to have some oranges in their hands, they flung them at the rider so adroitly that two of them struck him full in the face.

"Laugh, you wretches!" cried Zerbino, shaking his fist at them, "and may you keep on laughing till your teeth are worn to the gums."

And, behold, the two women laughed convulsively without stopping either for the threats of the wood-cutter or the commands of the princess, who pitied the poor churl.

"Good little woman!" said Zerbino, looking at Leila, "so sweet and so sad; I wish you nothing but good-luck. May you love the first man that makes you laugh, and marry him into the bargain."

Upon which he pulled his forelock, and bowed to the princess in the most gracious manner imaginable.

As a general rule, when one is astride a bundle of fagots it is better to bow to no one, not even a queen. Zerbino forgot this, to his sorrow. In order to salute the princess, he let go the rope that held the bundle together, when, behold, the sticks fell apart, and the honest Zerbino tumbled backward, his feet in the air, in the most grotesque way imaginable. He made a bold somersault, carrying with him half the leaves, and, crowned like a sylvan god, rolled over once more on the ground.

Why do we always laugh when a person falls at the risk of breaking his neck? I know not; it is a mystery which philosophy has not yet solved. What I do know is that every one laughed on that occasion, the Princess Leila like the rest. But she instantly sprang up, gazed at Zerbino with a peculiar expression, laid her hand on her heart and then on her head, and went in-doors, strangely agitated.

Meanwhile Zerbino gathered up the scattered sticks, and returned home on foot, like a simple woodman. Prosperity had not dazzled him, neither was he cast down by ill-luck. He bought a good Italian cheese, as white and hard as marble, cut a large slice from it, and dined with a hearty appetite. The poor simpleton little suspected what harm he had wrought, and what trouble he had left behind him.

"The sticks fell apart, and the honest Zerbino tumbled backward."

6*

V.

While these grave events were taking place, four o'clock struck in the tower of Salerno. The day was sultry, and silence reigned in the streets. Secluded in a lower chamber, far from the heat and noise, King Mouchamiel was dreaming of the happiness of his people—he was asleep.

All at once he awoke with a start. A pair of snowy arms were wound around his neck, and his face was wet with scalding tears. The fair Leila was embracing her father in a paroxysm of tenderness.

"What does this mean?" said the king, surprised at this outburst of affection. "What signify these kisses and tears? Child of your mother, you are trying to coax something out of me."

"On the contrary, my dear father, your obedient daughter has come to tell you that she is ready to follow your will.

I have found the son-in-law you have been seeking, and to please you will give him my hand."

"Good!" said Mouchamiel; "so this is the end of your whims. Who is it that you are going to marry? Is it the Prince of Cava? No. The Count of Capri, or the Marquis of Sorrento? No. Who is it, then?"

"I do not know, father."

"What! you do not know! You must have seen him, however?"

"Yes, just now, in the palace square."

"And did he speak to you?"

"No, father, what need is there of words, when hearts understand each other?"

Mouchamiel made a grimace, rubbed his ear, and, peering at his daughter through his half-closed eyelids, asked,

"At least, he is a prince?"

"I do not know, father; but what matters it?"

"It matters a great deal, my daughter. You know nothing of politics. You are free to choose any son-in-law that suits me, and it will be all right. As a king and a father, I will never interfere with your will while it agrees with mine. But otherwise, I have duties to fulfil towards my family and subjects; and I intend that my will shall be done. Where is this fine fellow, whom you do not know, who has never spoken to you, and who adores you?"

"I do not know."

"This is too much!" cried Mouchamiel. "Is it to talk such nonsense that you come hither to rob me of moments that belong to my people? Ho, there, chamberlains! Call the princess's women, and let them take her back to her apartments."

On hearing these words Leila raised her arms to heaven, burst into tears, and fell at the king's feet, sobbing. At the same moment the two women entered, still laughing ready to split their sides.

"Silence, wretches, silence !" exclaimed Mouchamiel, indignant at this lack of respect.

But the more the king cried silence the louder the women laughed, regardless of etiquette.

"Guards !" said the king, beside himself, "seize these insolent women and cut off their heads. I will teach them that there is nothing less laughable than a king."

"Sire !" said Leila, clasping her hands, "remember that you have rendered your reign illustrious by abolishing the penalty of death."

"You are right, my daughter. We are a civilized people. We will spare these women, and content ourselves with treating them in the Russian fashion with all possible consideration. Let them be knouted till they die a natural death."

"Pardon, father, pardon," said Leila. "It is your daughter that entreats you."

"For heaven's sake, let them stop laughing, and rid me of their presence," cried the good Mouchamiel. "Take away these idiots. I forgive them. Shut them up in a cell, till they die of silence and *ennui.*"

"Oh, father !" said poor Leila.

"Begone !" said the king; "marry them, and let that end the matter."

"Thanks, sire ! We shall laugh no longer," cried the two women, as they fell on their knees, opening their mouths and showing their toothless gums. "We are the victims of an infernal art; a wizard has bewitched us."

"A wizard in my state !" cried the king, who was a freethinker. "It is impossible ; there are none ; I do not believe in them."

"Sire," said one of the women, "is it natural for a bundle

of fagots to trot like a horse, and prance under the rein of a wood-cutter? This is what we have just seen in the square before the palace."

"A bundle of fagots!" returned the king. "That looks like witchcraft. Guards, seize the man and his fagots, and let them both be burned. After that I hope I shall be suffered to sleep in peace."

"Burn my beloved!" exclaimed the princess, tossing her arms like a sibyl. "Sire, this noble knight is my husband, my love, my life! Let a hair of his head be touched and I shall die."

"My household has gone distracted," said poor Mouchamiel. "What is the use of being king if I cannot even take an afternoon nap. It is all my good-nature. Call Mistigris! Since I have a minister, the least that he can do is to tell me what to think, and let me know what to wish."

VI.

Signor Mistigris was announced.
He was a little man; fat, short, round, and broad, who rolled rather than walked. Weasel eyes, looking every way at once, a low forehead, hooked nose, fat cheeks, and a triple chin: such was the minister that made Salerno happy, in the name of King Mouchamiel. He entered, simpering, puffing, and mincing like a man who lightly bears the weight of power.

"Here you are at last!" said the prince. "How is it that strange things take place in my dominions, and I, the king, am the last to be informed of them?"

"Everything is going on as usual," said Mistigris, calmly.

"I have the police reports here; peace and happiness prevail throughout the state," and he opened a large packet of papers and read as follows:

"Report of the Port of Salerno. All is tranquil. No more frauds in the custom-house than usual. Three quarrels between sailors, six stabs; five admissions to the hospital. Nothing new.

"City Report. Taxes doubled; prosperity and morality continually on the increase. Two women dead of hunger; ten foundlings; three men who have beaten their wives; ten wives who have beaten their husbands; thirty robberies; two assassinations; three poisonings. Nothing new."

"Is that all you know about it?" cried Mouchamiel, in an angry tone. "Well, sir, though it is not my business to be informed of the affairs of state, I know more about them than you do. A man has ridden through the square on a bundle of fagots, and bewitched my daughter. Here she is, wishing to marry him."

"Sire," said Mistigris, "I was not ignorant of this incident. A minister knows everything; but why trouble your majesty with such trifles? The man will be hung, and there will be an end of the matter."

"And can you tell me where this wretch is to be found?"

"Doubtless, sire!" replied Mistigris; "a minister sees everything, hears everything, and is present everywhere."

"Well, sir," said the king, "if in a quarter of an hour this fellow is not here, you will leave the ministry to those who are not content with seeing, but who also act. Begone!"

Mistigris left the room, still smiling. But, once in the anteroom, he turned purple with excitement, and was forced to cling to the arm of the first man he met. This was the prefect of the city, whom a happy chance threw in his way. Mistigris drew back and seized the magistrate by the collar.

"Sir!" said he, emphasizing each of his words, "if in ten minutes you do not bring me the man who rides through Salerno on a bundle of fagots, I will dismiss you. Do you understand? I will dismiss you. Begone!"

Stunned by this threat, the prefect ran to the chief of police.

"Where is the man that rides a bundle of fagots?" said he.

"What man?" asked the chief of police.

"Do not argue with your superior. I will not endure it. By not arresting this rascal you have utterly failed in your duty. If this man is not here in five minutes, I shall discharge you. Begone!"

The chief hastened to the police station, where he found the men set to watch over the public safety playing dice.

"You knaves!" he cried. "If in three minutes you do not bring me the man who rides a bundle of fagots, I will bastinado you like galley-slaves. Begone without a word."

The men went out cursing, while the wise and able Mistigris, confiding in the miracles of hierarchy, tranquilly returned to the king's chamber, recalling to his lips that perpetual smile which formed a part of his profession.

VII.

Two words whispered by the minister into the king's ear delighted Mouchamiel. The idea of burning a wizard was not displeasing to him. It was a striking little event that would do honor to his reign, a proof of wisdom that would astonish posterity.

One thing alone embarrassed the king, namely, poor Leila, who was drowned in tears, and whom her women vainly attempted to drag to her apartments.

Mistigris winked at the king, then approaching the princess, said, in his least surly tones:

"Madam, he is coming, and he must not find you in tears. Adorn yourself, on the contrary, be more beautiful than ever, and let the very sight of you assure him of his happiness."

"I understand you, good Mistigris," exclaimed Leila. "Thanks, my dear father, thanks," she added, seizing her father's hands, and covering them with kisses. "Bless you, bless you a thousand times!"

She went out intoxicated with joy, with head erect, eyes sparkling, and so happy that she stopped the first chamberlain on her way to inform him herself of her marriage.

"My good chamberlain," she added, "he is coming. Do the honors of the palace yourself, and be sure that we shall not be ungrateful."

Left alone with Mistigris, the king looked at his minister angrily.

"Are you mad?" he cried. "What! without consulting me, do you pledge my word? Do you think yourself the master of my empire, that you dispose of my daughter and me without my consent?"

"Bah!" said Mistrigris, tranquilly. "The first thing to be done is to calm the princess. In politics one never troubles himself about the morrow. 'Sufficient unto the day is the evil thereof.'"

"But my word!" resumed the king. "How can I break it without perjuring myself? I will have revenge on that insolent fellow who has stolen my daughter's heart."

"Sire," said Mistigris, "a prince never breaks his word; but there are several ways of keeping it."

"What do you mean by that?" asked Mouchamiel.

"Your majesty," continued the minister, "has just promised your daughter that she shall be married; we will marry her, after which we shall obey the law, which decrees,

"'If a noble under the rank of a baron dares pretend to

the love of a princess of royal blood, he shall be treated like a noble, that is, decapitated.

"'If the suitor is a citizen, he shall be treated like a citizen, that is, hung.

"'If he is a peasant, he shall be drowned like a dog.'

"You see, sire, that nothing is easier than to harmonize your paternal love and your royal justice. We have so many laws in Salerno that one can always be found to suit our case."

"Mistigris," exclaimed the king, "you are a scoundrel!"

"Sire," said the fat man, "you flatter me! I am nothing but a politician. I have been taught that there is one kind of morality for princes and another for the people, and I have profited by the lesson. It is this discernment which makes the genius of a statesman the admiration of the astute and the scandal of fools."

"My good friend," said the king, "with your long-winded phrases, you are as tiresome as an academical eulogy. I do not ask you for words, but for deeds; make haste to punish this man and let us have done with the matter."

As he was speaking, the Princess Leila entered the royal chamber. She was so beautiful, and her eyes shone with such joy, that the good Mouchamiel sighed, and began to wish that the rider of the fagots might be a prince, so that he should not be hung.

VIII.

Glory is a fine thing, but it has its disadvantages. Its possessor must bid farewell to the pleasure of living unknown and defying the silly curiosity of the crowd. The triumphal entry of Zerbino was not finished before every child in Salerno was acquainted with his person, home, and mode of life. The guards had little trouble, therefore, in finding the man they sought.

Zerbino was on his knees in the courtyard, busied in sharpening his famous axe. He was just trying the edge with his thumb-nail when a hand laid hold of his collar and set him on his feet. Half a score of kicks and a score of cuffs propelled him into the street. It was in this way that he learned that a minister was interested in his person, and that the king himself deigned to invite him to the palace.

Zerbino was a philosopher, and a philosopher is astonished at nothing. He thrust his hands into his pockets and walked on quietly, without troubling himself about the hail of blows that fell upon him. Nevertheless, a philosopher is not always a saint. A kick in the thigh wore out the patience of the wood-cutter.

"Gently!" said he; "have a little pity on a poor man!"

"I believe that the simpleton is arguing," said one of his

tormentors. "Our gentleman is made of down; we must handle him with gloves."

"I wish you were in my place," said Zerbino. "We should see whether you would laugh."

"Hold your tongue, you scoundrel," said the leader of the band, as he dealt him a blow that might have felled an ox.

The blow was badly aimed, doubtless, for instead of striking Zerbino, it went straight into the eye of one of the guards. Furious, and half blinded, the wounded man threw himself on the awkward fellow who had struck him, and seized him by the hair. A scuffle ensued; the bystanders attempted to separate them; fisticuffs rained up and down, right and left, and a general affray followed, enlivened with the shrieks of women, cries of children, and barking of dogs. It became necessary, at last, to call in the patrol, to restore order by arresting assailants, defenders, and spectators.

Zerbino, still unmoved, was proceeding towards the castle, when he was accosted, in the square, by a file of well-made fellows in embroidered coats and short breeches. They were the valets of the king, who, by the direction of the major-domo and the grand chamberlain himself, had come to meet the betrothed of the princess. Having been instructed to be polite, each one had his hat in his hand and a smile on his lips. They bowed to Zerbino. The wood-cutter, like a well-bred man, returned the salute. They bowed anew, and Zerbino again returned it; a performance which was repeated eight or ten times in succession with unmoved gravity. Zerbino was the first to tire; not having been born in the palace, his back was less supple than theirs; he was not accustomed to bending it.

"Stop!" he cried; "enough! three refusals are a sign of good-luck, and three bows are a sign of a dance. You have

bowed long enough, now dance." And, lo! the valets began to dance and bow, and to bow and dance, and, preceding Zerbino in admirable order, gave him an entrance into the castle worthy of a king.

IX.

To give himself a majestic air, Mouchamiel was gravely staring at the end of his nose, Leila was sighing, Mistigris was whittling a quill, like a diplomatist in search of an idea, and the courtiers, motionless and mute, seemed lost in contemplation. At last the great door of the saloon opened: the major-domo and valets entered with a measured tread, dancing a saraband which greatly surprised the court. Behind them walked the wood-cutter, as little moved by the royal splendors as if he had been born in a palace. Nevertheless, at the sight of the king, he stopped, took off his hat, and, clasping it in both hands to his breast, bowed three times, stretching out his right foot, after which he put on his hat again, seated himself calmly in an arm-chair, and crossed his legs.

"My father!" cried the princess, throwing herself on the king's neck, "this is the husband that you have given me. How handsome and noble he is! Do you not love him?"

"Mistigris," murmured Mouchamiel, half strangled, "question this man with the greatest respect. Think of my daughter's repose and my own. What luck! Oh, how happy fathers would be if they had no children!"

"Your majesty may be tranquil," said Mistigris; "humanity is my duty and pleasure."

"Up, scoundrel!" said he, harshly, turning to Zerbino, "answer quickly if you wish to save your skin. Are you a prince in disguise? You are silent, wretch! You are a wizard!"

"I am no more a wizard than you are, my fat fellow," answered Zerbino, without stirring from his chair.

"You villain!" exclaimed the minister, "your denial proves your crime, your silence proclaims you guilty."

"If I confessed should I be innocent?" asked Zerbino.

"Sire!" said Mistigris, who mistook rage for eloquence; "do justice, purge your state, purge the earth of this monster. Death is too mild a punishment for such a ruffian."

"Go on!" said Zerbino. "Bark! my fat fellow, bark! but don't bite."

"Sire!" said Mistigris, puffing and panting, "your justice and humanity are at stake: *bow, wow, wow.* Humanity commands you to protect your subjects by delivering them from this wizard: *bow, wow, wow*; justice demands that he should be hung or burned: *bow, wow, wow.* You are a father, *bow, wow,* but you are a king, *bow, wow,* and the king, *bow, wow,* should take precedence of the father, *bow, wow, wow.*"

"Mistigris," said the king, "you speak well, but your stammer is unbearable. Don't be so affected. Have done!"

"Sire!" screamed the minister, "death to the villain; the halter or the stake. *Bow, wow, wow.*"

While the king sighed, Leila, suddenly quitting her father, placed herself by Zerbino's side.

"Give your commands, sire!" said she. "This is my husband; his fate shall be mine."

At this shameless speech, all the court ladies covered their faces; Mistigris himself thought it incumbent upon him to blush.

"Unhappy girl!" cried the king, in a frenzy of rage; "by dishonoring yourself, you have pronounced your doom. Guards! seize these two creatures; let them be married on the spot; then confiscate the first boat that you find in the port, thrust these wretches into it, and abandon them to the waves."

"Oh, sire!" cried Mistigris, as the guards were dragging away the princess and Zerbino, "you are the greatest king on earth. Your goodness, gentleness, and indulgence will be the example and astonishment of posterity. In what language will the *Official Gazette* narrate it to-morrow! As for us, confounded by such magnanimity, we can only admire it in silence."

"My poor daughter," exclaimed the king, "what will become of her without her father? Guards! seize Mistigris, and put him, too, in the boat. It will be a consolation to me to know that so able a man is with my dear Leila. And then, to change ministers is always diverting, and in my sad condition I need something of the sort. Farewell, my good Mistigris."

Mistigris stood with his mouth wide open. He had just recovered breath enough to curse princes and their ingratitude when he was dragged from the palace. In spite of his prayers, threats, and tears he was thrust into the boat, and the three friends soon found themselves alone on the waters.

As to the good king Mouchamiel, he wiped away a tear, and shut himself up in his chamber to finish the nap so rudely interrupted.

"Zerbino held the rudder, and murmured some plaintive song."

X.

The night was calm and beautiful ; the moon shed its silver light on the sea, and over its tremulous waters ; the wind from the land drove on the bark, and already Capri was seen rising from the waves like a basket of flowers. Zerbino was at the helm, murmuring some plaintive woodman's or sailor's song. Leila sat at his feet, silent, but not sad. She was listening to her beloved. The past she had forgotten, for the future she had little care ; to stay by Zerbino's side was life to her.

Mistigris, less tender, was less of a philosopher. Restless and angry, he bustled about like a bear in its cage, and made fine speeches to Zerbino, to which the wood-cutter paid no heed, but only nodded, stolid as ever. Unaccustomed to official harangues, the orations of the minister put him to sleep.

"What will become of us ?" cried Mistigris. "Wretched wizard, if you have any power show it, and come to our rescue. Make yourself prince or king somewhere, and appoint me your prime-minister. I must have something to rule. What is the use of having power if you do not make your friends' fortune ?"

"I am hungry," said Zerbino, half opening his eyes.

Leila sprang up instantly, and began to look around her.

"My love," said she, "what would you like ?"

"Some figs and raisins," said the wood-cutter.

Mistigris uttered a cry ; a barrel of figs and raisins sprung up between his legs and threw him down.

"Oh !" thought he, springing up, "I know your secret, accursed wizard. If you can have what you wish for, my fortune is made ; I have not been minister for nothing, handsome prince, and I will make you wish for whatever I do."

While Zerbino was eating his figs Mistigris approached him, bowing and smiling.

"Signor Zerbino," said he, "I entreat of your excellency your incomparable friendship. Perhaps your excellency has not understood all the devotion that was hidden under the affected harshness of my words, but I assure you that it was planned the more speedily to insure your happiness. It was I alone that hastened your happy marriage."

"I am hungry," said Zerbino. "Give me some figs and raisins."

"Here they are, my lord," said Mistigris, with all the grace of a courtier. "I hope his excellency will be satisfied with my humble services, and will often permit me to display my zeal.

"Brute!" he murmured to himself, "you do not even listen to me. I must win Leila's favor at all hazards. The great secret of politics is to know how to please the ladies.

"By the way, Signor Zerbino," resumed he, simpering, "you forget that you were married this evening. Ought you not to make a wedding-gift to your royal bride?"

"A wedding-gift! you tire me, my fat fellow," answered Zerbino. "Where do you expect me to find such a thing? Go and bring me one from the fishes, at the bottom of the sea?"

At that very instant, as if hurled by an invisible hand, Mistigris leaped overboard and disappeared under the waves.

Zerbino set to work anew to stone and munch his raisins, while Leila never tired of watching him.

"There is a porpoise coming to the surface," said Zerbino.

It was not a porpoise, but the happy messenger, who had risen to the top and was struggling with the waves. Zerbino

seized him by the hair and pulled him into the boat.
Strange to say, Mistigris held in his teeth a carbuncle, that
shone like a star in the darkness.

"Here is the gift sent to the charming Leila by the king
of the fishes," stammered he, as soon as he could breathe.
"You see, Signor Zerbino, that you have in me the most
faithful and devoted of slaves. If ever you have a little
ministry to intrust to me—"

"I am hungry," interrupted Zerbino; "give me some figs
and raisins."

"My lord," resumed Mistigris, "will you do nothing for
your wife, the princess? This boat, exposed to the changes
of the weather, is not a fitting abode for one so young and
lovely."

"Hush, Mistigris," said Leila. "I am comfortable here.
I ask for nothing more."

"Do you remember, madam?" said the officious minister.

"that when the Prince of Capri offered you his hand he sent to Salerno a splendid ship of mahogany inlaid all over with gold and ivory, with sailors dressed in velvet, silken cordages, and three saloons adorned with mirrors. That is what a petty prince did for you. Signor Zerbino, noble, powerful, and good as he is, surely will not be left in the background."

"The man is a fool," said Zerbino; "he talks all the time. I should like to have such a vessel as that if only to stop your mouth, you chatterbox, and make you hold your tongue."

And lo! Leila uttered a cry of surprise and delight that made the woodsman start. He was on board a magnificent ship, that cleft the waves with the grace and majesty of a stately swan. A tent lighted with alabaster lamps formed a richly furnished drawing-room on deck. Leila, still seated at her husband's feet, gazed at him with admiration. Mistigris ran after the crew, and tried to give orders to all the sailors. But on this strange vessel no one said a word. Mistigris wasted his eloquence, and could not even find a cabin-boy to rule. Zerbino rose to look at the wake of the ship; and Mistigris ran after him, simpering.

"Is your lordship satisfied with my efforts and zeal?" asked he.

"Hold your tongue, you chatterer," said the woodsman. "I forbid you to say another word till morning. I am drowsy, let me go to sleep."

Mistigris stood with his mouth open, making respectful gestures; then in despair he went below to the dining-room and ate his supper in silence. He drank for four hours without being able to console himself, and ended by falling under the table. In the meantime Zerbino dreamed at his ease.

Leila alone did not close her eyes.

XI.

One tires of everything, even of happiness, says the proverb. With much greater reason might one tire of being at sea in a ship where no one said a word and which was drifting none knew whither. As soon, therefore, as Mistigris had regained his senses and speech, his sole idea was to persuade Zerbino to wish to be on land. The task was difficult. The adroit courtier was in constant fear that some indiscreet wish might send him again among the fishes; he trembled, above everything, lest Zerbino should regret his axe and forest. What a fate, to become the minister of a woodcutter!

Happily, Zerbino awakened in excellent humor. He was becoming accustomed to the princess, and her charming face pleased him, churl as he was. Mistigris wished to improve the occasion, but women, alas! are so unreasonable when they are in love! Leila declared to Zerbino that it would be sweet to live alone together, far from the world, in some tranquil cottage in an orchard, on the banks of a stream. Without understanding anything of this poetry, the honest Zerbino listened with pleasure to her loving words.

"A cottage with cows and chickens," said he, "that would be fine, if—"

Mistigris felt himself lost, and struck a decisive blow.

"Oh, my lord!" he cried, "look yonder before you. How beautiful that is!"

"What?" asked the princess; "I see nothing."

"Nor I either," said Zerbino, rubbing his eyes.

"Is it possible?" resumed Mistigris, with an air of astonishment. "What! do you not see that marble palace gleaming in the sun, and that stately staircase shaded with orange-trees, with its hundred steps leading down to the sea-shore?"

"A palace?" said Leila, "I want none; to live surrounded with courtiers, selfish followers, and valets. Let us fly!"

"Yes," said Zerbino. "A cottage is better; we should be quieter there."

"But this palace is unlike any other," exclaimed Mistigris, his imagination excited by his fears. "In this fairy abode there are neither courtiers nor valets; you are served by invisible hands, and are at once alone and surrounded by attendants. The furniture has hands, and the walls have ears."

"Have they a tongue?" said Zerbino.

"Yes," returned Mistigris, "they tell you everything you wish to know, but only speak at your bidding."

"Well," said the wood-cutter, "they have more wit than you. I should like to have such a castle as that. Where is this fine palace? I do not see it."

"It is there before you, my love," exclaimed the princess.

The vessel had made for land, and anchored in a harbor just deep enough for it to come up to the pier. The harbor was half surrounded by a great staircase of wrought iron. At the head of this staircase, overlooking the sea, on a vast plateau, arose the most charming palace that ever was seen.

The three friends gayly mounted the staircase, Mistigris at the head, puffing and blowing at every step. On reaching the gate of the castle he attempted to ring, but there was no bell; he called, and the gate itself answered.

"What do you want, stranger?" it asked.

"To speak with the master of this palace," said Mistigris, a little embarrassed at talking for the first time to a gate.

"The master of this palace is Signor Zerbino," replied the gate. "I will open to him when he appears."

Zerbino came up, with the fair Leila on his arm; the gate opened respectfully, and let the pair pass, followed by Mistigris.

Once on the terrace, Leila gazed with delight at the mag-

nificent spectacle of the vast sea glittering in the morning sun.

"How pleasant it is here," said she, "and how delightful it would be to sit in this gallery, under the shade of the blossoming laurels."

"Well," said Zerbino, "we can sit on the ground."

"Are there no easy-chairs here?" exclaimed Mistigris.

"Here we are! here we are!" cried the easy-chairs, and they hurried up, one after another, as fast as their four feet could carry them.

"This is a nice place to breakfast in," said Mistigris.

"Yes," returned Zerbino, "but where is the table?"

"Here I am! here I am!" answered a contralto voice, and a beautiful mahogany table, marching with matronly gravity, strode forward and placed itself before the guests.

"This is charming," exclaimed the princess, "but where is the food?"

"Here I am! here I am!" cried a number of little shrill voices, and thirty platters, followed by their sisters, the plates, and their cousins, the knives and forks, without forgetting their aunts, the salt-cellars, ranged themselves on the table, which was covered with game, fruit, and flowers.

"Signor Zerbino," said Mistigris," you see what I have done for you. All this is my work."

"You lie!" cried a voice.

Mistigris turned around, but saw no one. It was one of the pillars of the gallery that had spoken.

"My lord," said he, "no one can accuse me of imposture. I have always spoken the truth."

"You lie!" said a voice.

"This palace is detestable," thought Mistigris. "If the walls speak the truth, we shall never have a court here, and I shall never be minister. We must change this."

"Signor Zerbino," he resumed, "instead of living here alone, would you not rather be a king, and have subjects to pay you taxes, furnish you with soldiers, and surround you with love and tenderness?"

"Be a king—what good would that do me?" replied Zerbino.

"My friend, do not listen to him," said Leila. "Let us stay here; we are so happy, we two alone."

"We three," cried Mistigris; "I am the happiest of men here, and with you I desire nothing more."

"You lie!" said a voice.

"What, my lord, is there any one here that dares doubt my devotion?"

"You lie!" returned the echo.

"My lord, do not listen to this," exclaimed Mistigris. "I honor and love you; I swear it."

"You lie!" repeated the pitiless voice.

"Oh! if you do nothing but lie, begone to the moon," said Zerbino, "it is the land of liars."

It was an imprudent speech, for instantly Mistigris shot into the air, and disappeared above the clouds. Whether he ever descended again to earth no one knows, though some chroniclers say that he has since been seen there under another name. It is certain that he was never more beheld in a palace where the very walls spoke the truth.

XII.

Left alone, Zerbino folded his arms and looked at the sea, while Leila abandoned herself to the sweetest thoughts. To live in an enchanted solitude alone with one we love is the dream of our happiest days. She took Zerbino's arm and together they surveyed their new domain. On the right and left, the palace was surrounded with beautiful meadows watered with sparkling streams. Shady trees, purple beeches, larches with feathery cones, and fragrant orange-trees cast lengthening shadows over the turf. Among the foliage warbled the linnet, breathing joy and repose. Leila laid her hand on her heart, and, looking at Zerbino,

" My love," said she, " are you happy here, and have you nothing more to wish for ?"

" I have never wished for anything," said Zerbino. " To-morrow I shall take my axe and set to work ; there are fine forests to cut down here, and I can get plenty of fagots."

" Oh !" said Leila, sighing, " you do not love me."

" Love you !" exclaimed Zerbino, " what is that ? I wish you no harm, certainly ; quite the contrary. Here is a palace fallen from the clouds ; it is yours. Write to your father and tell him to come hither ; I shall be glad to see him. If I have hurt your feelings it was not my fault, I did not mean to. A wood-cutter I was born, and a wood-cutter I shall die. I was brought up to it, and I know how to keep my place. Don't cry ; I don't want to say anything to grieve you."

" Oh, Zerbino !" cried poor Leila, " what have I done that you should treat me so ? Am I so ugly and ill-tempered that you cannot love me ?"

" Love you ! I never thought of such a thing. There, there, don't cry, there is no use in it. Be calm, my child, be reasonable. What ! crying again. Well ! well ! I should like to love you, if it would give you pleasure. I do love you, Leila, I do love you !"

Poor Leila, bathed in tears, raised her eyes. Zerbino had undergone a transformation. In his glance she saw the tenderness of a husband—the devotion of a man who has given his heart and life forever to another. At the sight, Leila's tears flowed more freely than ever, but she smiled through them at Zerbino, who, for his part, wept for the first

time in his life. Is it not the greatest pleasure of earth to
shed tears without knowing why?

All at once, the fairy of the waters appeared, leading the
sage Mouchamiel by the hand. The good king had been
very unhappy since the loss of his daughter and his minister.
He embraced his children tenderly, gave them his blessing,
and bade them farewell the same day, in order to spare his
feelings and health. The fairy of the waters remained the
protectress of the spouses, who lived long in their beautiful
palace, happy in forgetting the world, and still happier in
being forgotten by it.

Did Zerbino remain a boor, like his father? Did his soul
ever open to the light of higher things? When he could un-
seal his mind with a word, was this word never whispered?
I know not, and am unable to conjecture. But what did it
matter, after all, since he was happy? He was beloved, and
that is the greatest joy of life. It was not necessary that he
should have wit; whether princess or shepherdess, every
woman in a household has wit enough for two.

THE SHEPHERD PACHA.

A TURKISH TALE.

ONCE upon a time there lived at Bagdad a pacha who
was greatly beloved by the sultan, and greatly dreaded by
his people. Ali, for this was the name of our friend, was a
true Mussulman, a Turk of the old school. As soon as the
dawn of day permitted him to distinguish a black thread
from a white one, he spread a carpet on the ground and, his
face turned towards Mecca, piously went through with his
ablutions and prayers. His devotions finished, two negro
slaves, dressed in scarlet, brought him his pipe and coffee,
when he settled himself on the divan, with his legs crossed,
and remained thus all day long. To sip black, bitter, and
scalding Mocha, smoke Smyrna tobacco slowly through a
long nargile, sleep, do nothing, and think less, such was his
fashion of governing. Every month, it is true, an order came
from Stamboul requiring him to send to the imperial treasury
a million of piasters, the taxes of the pachalic. The good
Ali, departing from his usual quiet, then summoned before

him the richest merchants of Bagdad, and politely asked them for two millions of piasters. The poor men raised their hands to heaven, beat their breasts, tore their beards, cast up their eyes, and swore that they had not a *para;* they implored pity of the pacha and mercy of the sultan. Upon which Ali, without ceasing to sip his coffee, ordered them to be bastinadoed on the soles of their feet till they brought this money which they did not possess, and which they always succeeded in finding somewhere. The sum counted out, the faithful administrator sent one half to the sultan and put the other into his own coffers, then again returned to his smoking. On these occasions he sometimes complained, despite his patience, of the cares of greatness and weariness of power; but the next day he thought no more of them, and levied the taxes the next month with the same calmness and disinterestedness. He was a model pacha.

Next to his pipe, coffee, and money, the thing dearest to Ali was his daughter, Delight-of-the-Eyes. He had reason to love her, for in his daughter as in a living mirror Ali saw himself reflected, with all his virtues. As indolent as she was beautiful, Delight-of-the-Eyes could not take a step without three women ready to wait on her: a white slave had charge of her hair and dress; a yellow slave held her mirror or fanned her, and a black slave amused her by her antics, and received her caresses or blows. The pacha's daughter drove out every morning in a great chariot, drawn by oxen; she spent three hours in the bath, and employed the rest of her time in making calls, munching rose conserves, drinking pomegranate sherbet, looking at dancing-girls, and ridiculing her dear friends. After a day so well spent she returned to the palace, kissed her father, and slept a dreamless slumber. Reading, thinking, embroidering, singing, and playing were tiresome tasks, which Delight-of-the-

Eyes took care to leave to her servants. When a girl is
young, beautiful, rich, and a pacha's daughter, she is born to
amuse herself, and what is there more amusing and more
praiseworthy than doing nothing. This is the way that the
Turks reason ; but how many Christians are Turks in this
respect?

There is no happiness here below without alloy ; were it
not so, earth would make us forget heaven. Ali experienced
this. One tax-day the vigilant pacha, less wide-awake than

usual, bastinadoed, by mistake, a Greek raya, a *protégé* of
England. The bastinadoed man clamored, as he had a right
to do, but the English consul, whose slumbers had been
broken, clamored louder than the raya, and England, who
never sleeps, clamored still more loudly than the consul.
She howled through the journals, vociferated in Parliament,
and shook her fist at Constantinople. The sultan grew
tired of so much fuss about such a trifle, and being unable to
rid himself of his faithful ally, of whom he stood in awe, he

determined at least to shake off the pacha, the innocent cause of all this hubbub. His highness's first idea was to strangle his late friend; but he reflected that to punish a Mussulman would give too much exultation and joy to those dogs of Christians, who were always barking. In his inexhaustible clemency, therefore, the Commander of the Faithful contented himself with ordering the pacha to be set on some desert shore and left to die of hunger.

Happily for Ali his judge and successor was an old pacha whose zeal was tempered by years, and who knew by experience that the will of sultans is immutable only in the almanac. He said to himself that his highness might some day regret his old friend, and would then give him credit for a clemency that cost him nothing. He caused Ali and his daughter to be brought to him in secret, gave them slaves' dresses and a few piasters, and warned them that if they were found in the pachalic the next day, or if he ever heard their names mentioned again, he would strangle or decapitate them, whichever they preferred. Ali thanked him for all his goodness, and an hour later was on his way with a caravan bound for Syria. That very evening the fall and exile of the pacha were proclaimed in the streets of Bagdad, and there was universal rejoicing. On all sides men extolled the justice and vigilance of the sultan, whose eyes were always open to the sufferings of his children. The next month, therefore, when the new pacha, whose hand was somewhat heavy, demanded two and a half million piasters, the good people of Bagdad paid it without grumbling, too happy at having escaped the claws of the brigand who for so many years had pillaged them with impunity.

To save one's head is fortunate, but it is not everything; it is necessary to live, and this is a somewhat difficult task for one accustomed to count upon the labor and money of óthers. On reaching Damascus, Ali found himself destitute of resources. A stranger, without friends or kinsmen, he was on the point of starving, and, what was still greater grief for a father, he saw his daughter growing pale and wasting away by his side.

What was he to do in this extremity? Ask alms? This was unworthy of a personage who the day before had a nation at his feet. Work? Ali had always lived like a nobleman; there was nothing that he knew how to do. His only secret of raising money had been to bastinado his fellows; but to exercise this respectable means of livelihood in peace it was necessary to be a pacha, and to have permission from the sultan. To carry it on as an amateur, at his own risk and peril, was to run the risk of being hung as a highway robber. Pachas dislike competition. Ali knew something about it; it had been the pride of his life from time to time to strangle some petty thief who had had the folly to poach upon rich men's domains.

Once day, when he had eaten nothing, and Delight-of-the-Eyes, worn out by long fasting, was unable to rise from the mat on which she lay, Ali, prowling around the streets of Damascus like a famished wolf, saw some men lifting jars of oil on their heads and carrying them to the warehouse near by. At the door of the warehouse stood a clerk who paid each porter a *para* for a jar. The sight of this little piece of copper made the ex-pacha's heart leap within him. He took his place in the line, and, mounting a narrow staircase, received a huge jar, which he had great difficulty in raising upon his back with both hands.

With rigid neck, elevated shoulders, and wrinkled brow Ali was slowly desending the stairs, when, at the third step, he felt his burden inclining forward. He threw himself back, his feet slipped, and he rolled to the bottom of the

staircase, followed by the jar, which broke in a thousand pieces, and deluged him with oil. He was rising, covered with shame, when the clerk of the warehouse seized him by the collar.

"Rascal!" said the latter, "pay me fifty piasters quickly, to repair your awkwardness, and begone; when a man knows nothing of a trade, he should let it alone."

"Fifty piasters!" said Ali, smiling bitterly. "Where do you expect me to get them? I have not a *para.*"

"If you do not pay with your purse you shall with your skin," returned the clerk. At a sign from him Ali was seized by four vigorous arms and flung on the ground, his feet were tied with ropes, and, in the attitude in which he had but too often placed others, he received fifty blows on his soles, as conscientiously applied as if a pacha had presided over the punishment.

He arose, lame and bleeding, wrapped his feet in some rags, and dragged himself home, sighing.

"God is great!" murmured he. "It is just that I should suffer myself what I have made others suffer. But the merchants of Bagdad whom I bastinadoed were happier than I; they had friends who paid for them, while I am famishing, and have nothing to reward me for my beating."

He was mistaken. A good woman, who, by chance or curiosity, had seen his mishap, took pity on him. She gave him oil to dress his wounds, a little sack of flour, and a few handfuls of pease on which to live till he was cured, and that night, for the first time since his fall, Ali could sleep without care for the morrow.

Nothing sharpens the wits like sickness and suffering. In his forced rest Ali was struck with a bright thought. "I was a fool," reflected he, "to undertake to be a porter. A pacha's strength does not lie in his muscles; to oxen belongs that honor. What distinguish men of my condition are skill and sleight of hand. I was an unequalled hunter, and, moreover, I know how to flatter and lie. I ought to know how, I have been a pacha. I will choose a business in which I can astonish the world by these brilliant qualities, and rapidly win an honorable fortune." Reflecting thus, Ali turned barber.

The first few days all went well. The master of the new barber made him draw water, scrub the shop, shake the rugs, keep the utensils in order, and serve the customers with coffee and pipes. Ali performed these delicate functions admirably. If by chance the head of some mountain peasant was intrusted to him, a wrong slip of the razor passed unnoticed: these good people are tough-skinned, and are not ignorant that they were made to be flayed; a little more or less does not affect them or rouse them from their torpor.

One morning, in the absence of the head barber, a great personage entered the shop, the very sight of whom intimidated poor Ali. It was the pacha's buffoon, a hideous little humpback with a head like a pumpkin, long hairy claws, a restless eye, and teeth like an ape. While Ali covered his face with a fragrant lather, the buffoon, leaning back in his chair, amused himself with pinching the new barber, laughing in his face, and running out his tongue at him. Twice he knocked from his hands the basin of suds, which delighted him to such a degree that he flung him four *paras*.

Nevertheless, the prudent Ali preserved his gravity. Absorbed in the care of so precious a face, he was guiding his razor with admirable regularity and lightness, when all at once the humpback made such a hideous grimace and uttered such a cry that the barber, frightened, suddenly drew back his hand, carrying away on the end of his razor half of an ear, and that not his own.

Buffoons like to laugh, but it is at the expense of others.

There are few men with thinner skins than those who chafe the skins of their neighbors. To fling himself on Ali and cuff and choke him, shouting murder meanwhile, was the humpback's first impulse. Happily for Ali, the cut was so deep that the wounded man was soon forced to think of his ear, from which a stream of blood was gushing. Ali seized the lucky moment and fled through the lanes of Damascus with the swiftness of a man who knows that to be caught is to be hung.

After many windings, he hid himself in a ruined cellar, and only ventured to return home in the darkness and silence of night. To stay at Damascus after such an accident was certain death. Ali had no difficulty in convincing his daughter that it was necessary to depart, and that at once. Their baggage was little encumbrance to them, and before dawn they had reached the mountain. For three days they walked without stopping, with nothing to eat but a few figs filched from the trees on the road, and a little water procured with great difficulty from the bottom of the dried-up ravines. But every misfortune has its compensation, and it must be said that never, in the times of their splendor, had the pacha or his daughter eaten or drunk with better appetite.

At their last stopping-place the fugitives were welcomed by an honest peasant who liberally practised the holy law of hospitality. After supper he talked with Ali, and, finding him without resources, offered to take him for a shepherd. To lead to the mountain a score of goats, followed by half a hundred sheep, was not a tiresome task; two good dogs did the hardest part of the work; he ran no risk of being beaten for his awkwardness; he had all the milk and cheese he wanted, and if the farmer did not give him a *para*, he at least permitted Delight-of-the-Eyes to take as much wool as she could spin, for her father's clothes and her own. Ali, who had no choice but to die of hunger or be hung, decided, without much reluctance, to lead the life of the patriarchs; the very next morning he made his way to the mountain with his daughter, his dogs, and his flock.

Once in the fields, Ali relapsed into his indolent ways. Stretched on his back smoking his pipe, he passed his time watching the flight of the birds through the air. Poor Delight-of-the-Eyes was less patient; she thought of Bagdad, and did not forget in her distaff the sweet leisure of olden times.

"My father!" she often said, "what is the use of life when it is nought but perpetual misery? Is it not better to put an end to it at once than to die by a slow fire?"

"God is great! my daughter," answered the wise shepherd; "what he does is well done. I have repose; at my age this is the chief of blessings; you see, therefore, that I am resigned. Ah! if I had only learned a trade. You have

"She was thinking of Bagdad, and her distaff did not make her forget the sweet leisure of other days."

youth and hope, and can look for a change of fortune. Are not these good reasons for taking comfort?"

"I am resigned, my good father," said Delight-of-the-Eyes, sighing. The more she hoped, the less was her resignation.

Ali had led this happy life in solitude for more than a year when one morning the son of the pacha of Damascus was hunting on the mountain. While chasing a wounded bird he lost his way. Alone, and far from his suite, he sought to find his path by following the course of a brook, when, on turning a rock, he saw before him a young girl sitting on the grass with her feet in the water, and braiding up her long hair. At the sight of this beautiful creature You-souf uttered a cry. Delight-of-the-Eyes raised her head. Terrified at the sight of a stranger, she fled to her father, and disappeared from the gaze of the astonished prince.

"Who can this be?" thought Yousouf. "The flower of the mountain is fresher than the rose of our gardens; this daughter of the desert is more beautiful than our sultanas. Here is the woman of whom I have dreamed."

He followed the steps of the unknown as fast as the slip-pery stones would let him, and at last found Delight-of-the-Eyes busied in milking the goats, while Ali called off the dogs, whose furious barking announced the stranger's ap-proach. Yousouf complained that he had lost his way and was dying of thirst. Delight-of-the-Eyes immediately brought him milk in a great earthen jug; he drank slowly, gazing at the father and daughter without speaking, and at last decided to ask his way. Ali, followed by his two dogs, con-ducted the hunter to the foot of the mountain and returned trembling; the stranger had given him a piece of gold; he must be an officer of the sultan, perhaps a pacha. To Ali, who judged from his own recollections, a pacha was a man who could only do harm, and whose friendship was to be dreaded quite as much as his hatred.

On reaching Damascus, Yousouf threw himself on his mother's neck: he repeated to her that she was as beautiful as at sixteen, and as brilliant as the moon in its full; that she was his only friend, and that he loved no one else in the world; saying which he kissed her hands again and again.

His mother smiled. "My child," said she, "you have a secret to confide to me; speak quickly. I know that I am not as beautiful as you call me, but I am sure of this, that you will never have a better friend than I."

Yousouf did not wait to be urged. He was burning to tell what he had seen on the mountain; he drew a marvellous portrait of the fair stranger, and declared that he could not live without her, and would marry her the next day.

"A little patience, my son!" said his mother. "Let us learn who this miracle of beauty is; after that we will persuade your father to give his consent to this happy marriage."

When the pacha learned of his son's passion, he began with expostulations and ended with a fit of rage. Were rich and elegant girls so scarce in Damascus that his son must go to the desert in search of a shepherdess? Never would he give his consent to this wretched marriage, never!

Never is a word which a prudent man should beware of speaking in his household when his wife and son are arrayed against him. A week had not passed before the pacha, moved by the mother's tears and the son's pallor, retired from the field, tired of the contest; but, like a strong-minded man who knows his own value, he openly declared that he was doing a foolish thing and that he knew it.

"All right!" said he; "let my son marry a shepherdess, if he will; his folly be on his own head; I wash my hands of him. But, that nothing may be lacking to this absurd marriage, let my fool come hither; he is the fitting messenger to send for this wretched goatherd who has bewitched my household."

An hour after the humpback, mounted on an ass, was on his way to the mountain, execrating the caprice of the pacha and the love of Yousouf. What sense was there in sending as ambassador to a shepherd, through dust and sun, a delicate man, born to live under the canopy of a palace and to delight lords and princes by the brilliancy of his wit? But, alas! fortune is blind; it seats fools on the pinnacle of power, and reduces geniuses who would not die of hunger to the condition of fools.

Three days of fatigue had not softened the ill-humor of the humpback, when he saw Ali lying in the shade of a tree, and more occupied with his pipe than his sheep. Giving his ass a kick, the fool advanced towards the shepherd with the majesty of a vizier.

"Fellow!" said he, "you have bewitched the pacha's son; he does you the honor to marry your daughter. Scour up this pearl of the mountain as quickly as you can, I must carry her back to Damascus. As for yourself, the pacha sends you this purse, and orders you to clear out of the country as fast as possible."

Ali let fall the purse that was flung him, and, without turning his head, asked the humpback what he wanted.

"Stupid brute!" returned the latter. "Didn't you hear me? The pacha's son takes your daughter in marriage."

"What does the pacha's son do for a living?" asked Ali.

"What does he do for a living?" cried the buffoon, bursting into a fit of laughter. "Blind dotard that you are, do you imagine that so exalted a personage as he is a rustic of your sort. Don't you know that the pacha shares the tithes of the provinces with the sultan, and that out of the forty sheep that you tend so badly, there are five that belong to him by right, and thirty-five that he can take if he chooses."

"I am not talking of the pacha," tranquilly returned Ali. "God protect his Excellency! I ask you what his son does for a living? Is he an armorer?

"No! you fool!"

"A blacksmith?"

"By no means!"

"A carpenter?"

"No!"

"A charcoal-burner?"

"No, nò; he is a great gentleman. Don't you know, you

blind bat, that nobody but beggars work? The son of the pacha is a noble lord; that is to say, he has white hands and does nothing."

"Then he shall not have my daughter," said the shepherd, gravely. "Housekeeping is expensive, and I will never give my daughter to a husband who cannot support his wife. But perhaps the pacha's son has some lighter trade. Is not he an embroiderer?"

"No," said the buffoon, shrugging his shoulders.

"A tailor?"

"No."

"A potter?"

"No."

"A basket-maker?"

"No."

"Is he a barber, then?"

"No," said the humpback, purple with rage; "stop this foolish jesting or I will have you beaten to a jelly. Call your daughter, I am in haste."

"My daughter shall not go," said the shepherd.

He whistled to his dogs, who gathered round him, growling, and showing fangs which appeared to give little amusement to the envoy of the pacha. He mounted his ass, and, shaking his fist at Ali, who held back his dogs, bristling with rage,

"Wretch!" said he, "you shall soon hear from me. You shall know what it costs to have any other will than that of the pacha, your master and mine."

The buffoon returned to Damascus with his maimed ear hanging lower than usual. Happily for him, the pacha took the matter in good part. It was a little disappointment for his wife and son, and a triumph for himself; a double success which agreeably tickled his pride.

8

"Upon my word!" said he, "the honest man is even madder than my son. But don't be troubled, Yousouf, a pacha never breaks his word. I will send four horsemen to the mountain to bring me the girl; as for the father, have no anxiety about him; I have a decisive argument in store for the fellow."

Saying this, he made an airy gesture with his hand, as if cutting down something that was in his way.

At a sign from his mother Yousouf arose, and entreated his father to leave to him the care of carrying out this little adventure. Doubtless the means proposed was irresistible, but Delight-of-the-Eyes might be weak enough to love the old shepherd; she would weep for him; and the pacha would not wish to sadden the honeymoon. Yousouf hoped, with a little persuasion, easily to overcome a resistance which seemed to him unreasonable.

"Very well," said the pacha. "You think yourself wiser than your father; it is the way with sons. Go, and do as you please; but I warn you that from this day forth I wash my hands of your affairs. If that old fool of a shepherd refuses you, that ends the matter. I would give a thousand piasters to see you return as discomfited as the humpback."

Yousouf smiled; he was sure of success. How could Delight-of-the-Eyes help loving him? He adored her. Moreover, at twenty, who doubts himself or his good fortune. Doubt is for those whom life has deceived, and not for those whom she intoxicates with her first illusions.

Ali received Yousouf with all the respect due to the son of a pacha. He thanked him politely for his honorable proposal, but continued inexorable. No trade—no marriage. It was for him to choose. The young man had thought that Delight-of-the-Eyes would come to his aid; but Delight-of-the-Eyes was invisible; and there was a good reason for her not disobeying her father ; the prudent Ali had not said a word to her about the marriage. Since the visit of the buffoon he had carefully kept her shut up in the house.

The pacha's son returned from the mountain utterly cast down. What should he do? Return to Damascus to be the butt of his father's railleries? Never would Yousouf resign himself to this. Lose Delight-of-the-Eyes? Rather death. Make this old shepherd change his mind? Yousouf could not hope for it, and he almost came to the point of regretting that he had ruined his cause by too great kindness of heart.

Amid these sad reflections he suddenly perceived that his horse, left to himself, had strayed away. Yousouf found him on the edge of an olive wood. In the distance he spied a village. The bluish smoke rose above the roofs, and he heard the barking of dogs, the song of the workmen, and the noise of the forge and hammer. An idea struck Yousouf. What hindered him from learning a trade? Was it so very difficult? Was not Delight-of-the-Eyes worth any sacrifice? The young man tied his horse to an olive-tree, upon which he hung his weapons, embroidered jacket, and turban. At the first house he reached he complained of having been robbed by the Bedouins, bought a rough suit of clothes, and, thus disguised, went from door to door to offer himself as an apprentice. Yousouf's appearance was so prepossessing that every one welcomed him cordially, but he was appalled at the conditions proposed to him. The blacksmith asked two years to teach him, the potter one year, and the mason six months ; it was a century. The pacha's son would not resign himself to this long servitude. All at once a shrill voice called out : "Ho! my son, if you are in haste and are not ambitious, come with me ; in a week I will teach you how to earn your living."

Yousouf raised his head. A few steps from him a little
fat man with round belly and rosy face was seated on a
bench with his legs crossed ; he was a basket-maker. He
was surrounded with straw and reeds of all colors. With a
skilful hand he plaited the braids, which he then sewed together into baskets, mats, and hats of varied shades and pat-
terns. It was a charming sight.

"You are my master," said Yousouf, taking the hand of
the basket-maker ; "and if you can teach me your trade in

two days, I will pay you well for your pains. Here is my
advance fee."

With these words he flung two pieces of gold to the
amazed workman.

An apprentice who scatters gold about him is not seen
every day. The basket-maker did not doubt that he had to
deal with a prince in disguise. He did wonders, and, as his
pupil lacked neither intelligence nor good-will, before night
he had taught him all the secrets of his trade.

"My son," said he, "your education is finished ; you shall
judge before night whether your master has earned **his**

money. The sun is setting; it is the time when people pass my door on their way home from work. Take this mat, which you have braided and sewed with your own hands, and offer it for sale. Either I am greatly mistaken or you will sell it for four *paras*. For a beginner that is doing well."

The basket-maker was not mistaken. The first purchaser offered three *paras*. He was asked five, and after more than an hour's haggling he finally decided to give four. He drew out his long purse, looked several times at the mat, criticised it, and finally made up his mind to count out his four copper coins, one by one. But, instead of taking the money, Yousouf flung a piece of gold to the purchaser, and ten to the basket-maker; then, seizing his masterpiece, he rushed from the village like a madman. On reaching his horse he spread the mat on the ground, enveloped his head in his mantle, and slept the most restless but, nevertheless, the sweetest sleep that he had ever tasted in his life.

At daybreak, when Ali came to the pasture with his sheep, he was greatly astonished to see Yousouf installed before him under the old carob-tree. As soon as he perceived the shepherd, the young man arose, and, taking the mat on which he had been lying,

"My father!" said he, "you required me to learn a trade. I have done so. Here is my work, examine it for yourself."

"It is a fine bit of work," said Ali; "if it is not very smoothly braided, it is honestly sewed. What can you earn by making one mat a day like this?"

"Four *paras*," said Yousouf, "and with a little practice, I could make two at least in a day."

"Be modest," returned Ali; "modesty becomes youthful talent. Four *paras* a day is not much, but four *paras* to-day and four to-morrow make eight *paras*, and four *paras* the day after will make twelve. In fine, it is a trade at which a man can earn a living, and if I had had the wit to learn it when I was pacha, I should not have had to turn shepherd to-day."

These words filled Yousouf with astonishment. Ali told him his whole story. It was risking his head, but a little pride is excusable in a father on giving his daughter in marriage. Ali was not sorry to show his son-in-law that Delight-of-the-Eyes was not unworthy to be the wife of a pacha's son.

The sheep that day went home earlier than usual. Yousouf was anxious to thank the honest farmer who had given shelter to Ali and his daughter. He bestowed on him a purse of gold to reward him for his charity. None is so liberal as a happy man. Delight-of-the-Eyes, on being introduced to the mountain hunter, and informed of Yousouf's intentions, declared that it was a daughter's first duty to obey her father. In such cases, it is said, daughters are always obedient in Turkey.

The same day, in the cool of the evening, they set out for Damascus. The horses were fleet, and their hearts were light ; they went like the wind, and, before the close of the second day, they had reached their destination. Yousouf presented his bride to his mother. It is needless to say how great was her joy. After the first caresses, she could not resist the pleasure of showing her husband that she had been wiser than he, and took pleasure in revealing to him the birth of the fair Delight-of-the-Eyes.

" By Allah !" cried the pacha, stroking his long beard to keep himself in countenance, and hide his confusion, "do you imagine, madam, that you can surprise a statesman like me? should I ever have consented to this union if I had not known the secret that astonishes you? Understand that a pacha knows everything." And he instantly retired to his

study to write to the sultan, that he might decide Ali's fate. He was not ready to displease his highness for the bright eyes of an outlawed family. Youth loves romance in life, but the pacha was a serious man, who was anxious to live and die a pacha.

All sultans love stories, if we are to believe "The Thousand and One Nights." Ali's protector had not degenerated from his ancestors. He sent a ship expressly to Syria to bring the ex-pacha of Bagdad to Constantinople. Ali, clad in rags, with crook in hand, was led to the seraglio, where, before a numerous audience, he had the honor of amusing his majesty during a whole afternoon.

When Ali had finished his story, the sultan ordered him to be clothed in a robe of honor. Of a pacha his highness had made a shepherd; he wished now to astonish the world by a new miracle of his omnipotence, and of a shepherd to make a pacha.

The whole court applauded this brilliant mark of favor. Ali threw himself at the sultan's feet, and declined an honor which had lost all attractions for him. He did not wish, he said, to run the risk of displeasing the master of the world a second time, and begged to grow old in obscurity, blessing the generous hand that had rescued him from the abyss into which he had justly fallen.

Ali's boldness appalled the spectators, but the sultan smiled.

"God is great!" he cried, "and has some new surprise in store for us each day. During the twenty years that I have reigned, this is the first time that one of my subjects has asked to be nothing. For the rarity of the thing, Ali, I grant your prayer. All that I ask is that you shall accept a gift of a thousand purses. No one must leave my presence empty-handed."

On his return to Damascus Ali bought a beautiful garden, filled with oranges, lemons, apricots, plums, and grapes. To dig, hoe, graft, prune, and water these was his sole delight. He went to bed every night with a tired body and tranquil soul, and arose every morning refreshed and light-hearted.

Delight-of-the-Eyes had three sons, all more beautiful than their mother. Old Ali undertook to bring them up. He taught all of them gardening, and made each one learn a different trade. To engrave on their hearts the truth that he had learned only in exile, he inscribed on the walls of his house and garden the finest passages of the Koran, above which he wrote these wise sayings, which the Prophet himself would not have disowned :

"Labor is the only treasure that never fails us."

"Use thy hands for work and thou wilt never stretch them for alms."

"When thou knowest what it costs to earn a *para*, thou wilt respect others' property and labor."

"Work brings health, wisdom, and joy."

"Labor and dulness never dwell under the same roof."

It was amid such wise teachings that the sons of Delight-of-the-Eyes grew up. All three were pachas. Whether they profited by their grandfather's counsels I know not. I like to think so, although the annals of the Turks are silent concerning it. The first lessons of infancy are not forgotten. It is to education that we owe three fourths of our vices and half our virtues. Good people, remember what you owe to your fathers, and say to yourselves that wicked men and pachas, are, for the most part, only children badly trained.

8*

BRIAM THE FOOL.

AN ICELANDIC TALE.

I.

In the good country of Iceland, there once lived a king and queen who ruled a faithful and obedient people. The queen was good and gentle, and little attention was paid to her; the king was grasping and cruel, and all who feared him, therefore, vied with each other in praising his virtue and kindness. Thanks to his avarice, the king had more castles, farms, herds, goods, and jewels than he could count, but the more he had, the more he wanted. Woe to the man, rich or poor, who fell into his power!

At the lower end of the park about the royal castle stood a little hut, where dwelt an old peasant and his wife. Providence had bestowed on them seven sons, and these were all their riches. To feed this large family the good people had nothing but a cow, called Bukolla. She was a splendid animal, black-and-white, with short horns, and large, soft, and gentle eyes. Her beauty, moreover, was her very least merit; she was milked thrice a day, and never gave less than five gallons at a time. She was so devoted to her masters that she came home of her own accord at milking-time, dragging her full udders, and lowing from afar for them to come to her relief; in short, she was the delight of the household.

One day, as the king was hunting, he chanced to pass through the pasture where the cows of the castle were feeding. Unluckily, Bukolla had strayed among the herd.

"What a fine cow I have there!" exclaimed he.

"Sire," answered the herdsman, "it is not yours; it is Bukolla, the cow of the old peasant that lives in the hovel yonder."

"I must have her," said the king, and through the whole hunt he talked of nothing but Bukolla. At night, on his return, he called the captain of his guard, who was as wicked as himself, and said, "Go find that peasant, and bring me directly the cow that has struck my fancy."

The queen begged him to forbear. "These poor people," said she, "have nothing in the world but their cow; to take her away is to make them die of starvation."

"I must have her," returned the king, "by purchase, barter, or force, no matter which. If, in an hour, Bukolla is not in my stables, woe to the knave that has failed in his duty!" And he frowned so fiercely that the queen dared not open her lips, and the captain of the guard set off post-haste with a band of soldiers.

The peasant was milking the cow in front of the door, with all the children gathered round, caressing her. On hearing the king's message the good man shook his head, and declared that he would not sell Bukolla at any price. "She is mine," said he, "she is my joy and treasure, and I love her better than all the king's gold."

It was growing late, and the captain of the guard feared his master's wrath. He seized Bukolla by the horns to drag her away. The peasant sprang to his feet, to offer resistance, when a blow from an axe laid him dead on the ground. At the sight, all the children burst into tears except Briam, the eldest, who stood, pale and speechless, as if transfixed to the spot.

The captain of the guard knew that blood for blood is the law in Iceland, and that sooner or later the sons would avenge their father. If the tree was not to grow again, it must be plucked up, root and branch. With a frenzied grasp, the ruffian seized one of the crying children. "Where is your pain?" he asked. "Here," said the child, laying his hand on his heart, whereupon the wretch instantly plunged a dagger into his breast. Six times he put the same question and received the same answer, and six times he flung the corpse of the son upon that of the father. All this time, Briam, with his eyes and mouth wide open, was running about, chasing the flies as they buzzed in the air.

"Come here, you rascal! where is your pain?" cried the executioner.

For his sole answer, Briam put his thumb and forefinger to his nose in token of contempt, and ran off as fast as his legs could carry him, singing and dancing. The captain of the guard was about to pursue the insolent fellow, when he was stopped by his companions.

"Fie!" said they; "kill the cub after the wolf, but do not kill a fool! What harm can he do you?"

That evening the king had the pleasure of stroking Bukolla, and the thought never crossed his mind that she had cost him too dear. But in the ruined hovel an old woman, in tears, entreated justice of God. The whim of a prince had robbed her in an hour of her husband and six children. Of all whom she loved, of all who were her support, nought was left her but a wretched idiot.

II.

Ere long, nothing was talked of for twenty leagues round but Briam and his antics. One day, he wanted to drive a nail into the axle of the sun ; another, he tossed up his cap to the man in the moon. The king, who was ambitious, thought that it would be a good thing to have a fool at his court, in humble imitation of the great princes of the Continent. Briam was sent for, accordingly, and dressed in a motley suit, with one leg red and the other blue, one sleeve green and the other yellow ; and an orange body. In this parrot-like costume, he was set to amuse the courtiers. Sometimes caressed and oftener beaten, the poor fool suffered everything without complaint. He passed whole hours in talking with the birds or watching the

burial of an ant. If he opened his lips, it was to make some mad speech, which greatly delighted those who were not its butt.

One day, when dinner was about to be served, the captain of the guard entered the castle kitchen. Briam, armed with a chopping-knife, was cutting up carrot leaves in the style of parsley. The sight of the knife terrified the murderer, and aroused his suspicions. " Briam, where is your mother?" asked he.

" There she is, hanging yonder," answered the idiot, pointing with his finger at the huge pot, where the royal dinner was stewing.

" Stupid lout, what do you mean?" exclaimed the guardsman, opening his eyes.

" That is my mother; it is what feeds me," returned Briam. And, springing to the fireplace, he grasped the sooty pot in his arms, and ran off with it to the forest. They chased him, but it was labor lost ; when they caught him, the dinner was spilled and everything spoiled. That night the king was forced to dine on a crust of bread, and his only consolation was to have Briam soundly whipped by the scullions of the castle.

Briam limped to his mother's hovel, and told her what had happened. " My son, my son," said the poor woman, " that is not what you should have said."

" What should I have said, mother?"

" My son, you should have said, ' This is the pot that is filled every day by the king's generosity.' "

" Well, mother, I will say that to-morrow."

The next day the court was assembled. The king was talking with his high-steward—a great lord, who loved good cheer, fat, sleek, and jolly ; with a large, bald head, a thick neck, a huge belly, over which he could not cross his arms,

and a pair of little legs which with difficulty supported this
vast structure. As the steward was talking with the king,
Briam came up, and struck him a smart blow in the belly,
saying: " This is what is filled every day by the king's generosity."

It is needless to say
that a beating followed.
The king was furious,
and the court like-
wise ; but it was whis-
pered that evening
throughout the castle
that fools, without
knowing it, sometimes
speak the truth.

Briam limped to his
mother's hut, and told
her what had hap-
pened. "My son, my
son," said the poor
woman, " that is not
what you should have
said."

" What should I have said, mother ?"

" My son, you should have said, ' This is the best and
most faithful of courtiers.' "

" Well, mother, I will say that to-morrow."

The next day the king held a grand levée, and while the
ministers, officers, chamberlains, fine gentlemen, and fair
ladies were disputing the smiles of the monarch, he amused
himself by teasing a large spaniel that was trying to snatch
a cake from his hands.

Briam seated himself at the king's feet, and, seizing the

dog by the nape of the neck, causing it to howl piteously, cried, " This is the best and most faithful of courtiers."

The king smiled at this jest, upon which the courtiers all burst out laughing, but no sooner had he left the room than a shower of blows and kicks rained upon poor Briam, who had great difficulty in escaping the storm.   He limped to his mother's hut and told her what had happened.

" My son, my son," said the poor woman, "that is not what you should have said."

." What should I have said, mother ?"

" You should have said, ' This creature would eat up everything if one would let her.' "

" Well, mother, I will say that to-morrow."

The next day was a holiday, and the queen appeared in her most gorgeous array.   She was covered with velvet, laces, and jewels ; her necklace alone was worth the tax of twenty villages.   All admired her splendor. Just then Briam came up, crying, " This creature would eat up everything if one would let her."

It would have been all over with the insolent wretch if the queen herself had not interceded for him.

" Poor fool," said she, " begone ; no one shall hurt you. If you knew how these jewels weigh me down, you would not reproach me for wearing them."

Briam hastened to his mother's hut, and told her what had happened.   " My son, my son," said the poor woman, " that is not what you should have said."

" What should I have said, mother ?"

" My son, you should have said, ' This is the king's love and pride.' "

" Well, mother, I will say that to-morrow."

The next day, the king was going to the chase.   His favorite mare was brought him ; he mounted, and was carelessly bidding the queen good-bye, when Briam struck the horse on the shoulder, saying, " This is the king's love and pride."

The king looked angrily at Briam, upon which the poor fool ran off as fast as his legs could carry him, already beginning to scent the whip in the air. He entered his mother's hut, out of breath, and told her what had happened.

" My son," said the poor woman," do not go back to the castle ; they will kill you."

" Patience, mother, none can say who will slay and who will be slain."

" Alas !" said his mother, weeping; " how happy your father is to be in his grave, where he cannot see your shame and mine."

" Patience, mother, no two days are alike."

III.

Almost three months had passed since Briam's father slept in the grave with his children, when the king gave a great feast to the chief officers of his court. The captain of the guard sat at his right and the fat high-steward at his left. The table was covered with lights, fruits and flowers, and the guests quaffed the choicest wine from golden cups. As the drink went round their blood grew heated, words ran high, and more than one quarrel was threatening. Briam, madder than ever, poured the wine, and took care not to leave a glass empty, but while he held the golden flagon with one hand, with the other he pinned the clothing of the guests together, two by two, so that no one could rise without dragging his neighbor after him.

He had made the round of the board three times, when the king cried, heated with wine :

" Jump upon the table, fool, and give us a song !"

Briam leaped up lightly among the fruits and flowers, and began chanting in a mournful strain:

"Each has its turn,
Wind and rain,
Night and day,
Death and life,
Each has its turn."

"What do you mean by this dismal dirge?" exclaimed the king. "Fool, make me laugh or I will make you cry."

Briam looked at the king fiercely, and chanted, in a menacing voice:

"Each has its turn,
Good luck and ill,
Outrage and vengeance,
Deaf are the fates,
Each has its turn."

"What! villain, it looks as if you were threatening me," cried the king; "you shall be punished as you deserve."

He rose to his feet so suddenly that he dragged after him the captain of the guard. The latter, taken by surprise, fell forward, and, to steady himself, caught hold of the king's elbow and neck.

"Wretch!" cried the prince, "do you dare to lay hands on your master?" And, seizing his dagger, he was about to stab the officer when the latter grasped the king's arm with one hand, and, with the other, plunged his dirk into his throat. The blood gushed forth in torrents, and the prince fell, dragging his murderer with him in the death-struggle.

The captain of the guard rose quickly, amid shrieks and confusion, and, drawing his sword, exclaimed, "Gentlemen, the tyrant is dead. Hurrah for liberty. I will be king and will marry the queen. If any one objects, let him speak, I am ready for him."

"Long live the king!" cried all the courtiers; and there were even a few who took advantage of the occasion to draw a petition from their pockets. The joy was universal, and almost delirious. Suddenly, with flashing eyes and uplifted axe, Briam stood before the usurper.

"Dog, and son of a dog," he cried, "when you slew my kindred, you thought neither of God nor man. Your time has come!"

The captain of the guard attempted to draw his sword,

but Briam dealt his right arm such a blow that it fell like a broken bough.

"And now," cried Briam, "if you have a son, let him avenge you, as Briam this day avenges his father." With these words, he cleft his skull asunder.

"Long live Briam!" cried the courtiers; "long live our liberator!" At that instant the queen entered, terror-stricken, and threw herself at the fool's feet, calling him her avenger. Briam raised her from the ground, then, seating himself by her side and brandishing his axe, he called on all the courtiers to swear fidelity to their lawful sovereign.

"Long live the queen!" cried every one. The joy was universal and almost delirious.

The queen wished to keep Briam at the court; but he begged to return to his hut, and asked no other reward than the poor cow, the innocent cause of so much suffering. On approaching the door of the cottage, the cow began to low for those who could no longer hear her. The poor woman came out, in tears.

"Mother," said Briam, "here is Bukolla; you are avenged!"

"At that instant the queen entered, terror-stricken, and threw herself at the fool's feet."

Here ends the story. What became of Briam none can
tell ; but the whole country still points out the ruins of the
hut where he and his brothers dwelt, and mothers say to

their children, " There lived the lad who avenged his father
and comforted his mother." And the children answer,
" We will follow his example."

THE LITTLE GRAY MAN.

AN ICELANDIC TALE.

In olden times—I speak of three or four hundred years ago—there lived at Skalholt, in Iceland, an old peasant, who was no more richly endowed with wit than he was with money. One day, when the honest man was at church, he heard a fine sermon on charity. ' "Give alms, brethren, give alms!" said the curate, "and the Lord will restore it to you a hundred-fold." These words, which were repeated again and again, fixed themselves in the peasant's mind, and muddled what little brains he had. Scarcely had he returned home when he began to cut down the trees in his garden, dig up the ground, and fetch wood and stones, as if he were about to build a palace.

"What are you doing, my poor man?" asked his wife.

"Don't call me 'poor man' any longer," said the peasant, gravely; "we are rich, my dear wife, or, at least, we soon shall be. In a fortnight I am going to give away my cow."

"Our only means of livelihood," cried the wife; "we shall die of starvation."

"Hold your tongue, you ignoramus," said the peasant; "it is clearly to be seen that you did not listen to the curate's sermon. By giving away our cow we shall receive a hundred more as a reward; the curate said so, and it is gospel truth; I shall put fifty of them in the stable that I am going to build, and with the money that I get for the other fifty I shall buy meadow-land enough to keep our herd both in winter and summer. We shall be richer than the king." And, without troubling himself about either the prayers or reproaches of his wife, the simpleton went on building his stable, to his neighbors' great astonishment.

The work finished, he tied a rope around the cow's neck, and led her straight to the curate's house. He found him talking with two strangers, at whom he scarcely glanced, so eager was he to make his gift and to receive the promised reward. The curate was greatly astonished at this new form of charity. He made a long speech to his foolish sheep, to prove to him that our Lord had spoken of spiritual rewards alone; but it was sheer waste of time; the peasant only answered, "You said so, Mr. Curate; you said so." Tired, at last, of reasoning with such a dolt, the pastor fell into a fit of holy wrath, and shut his door in the face of the peasant, who stood in the road thunder-struck, repeating, "You said so, Mr. Curate; you said so."

Nothing was left for him but to return home; and this was not an easy matter. It was early spring; the ice was melting, and the gusts of wind blew the snow in all directions. He slipped at every step, while the cow lowed, and would not go on. At the end of an hour he had lost his way, and was in danger of losing his life. He stopped, perplexed, execrating his ill-fortune, and not knowing what to do with the animal that he was dragging along. As he was sadly reflecting, a man came up, carrying a huge sack, and asked him what he was doing abroad in such wretched weather.

The peasant told the story of his troubles. "My good man," said the stranger, "if you take my advice, you will make a trade with me. I live close by here ; give me your cow, which you can never get home, and take this sack, which is no more than you can carry, and which is full of good things ; it holds nothing but meat and bone."

The bargain struck, the stranger led away the cow, while the peasant threw over his shoulder the sack, which he found frightfully heavy. Dreading his wife's reproaches and ridicule, the instant he entered the house he hastened to tell of the danger he had run, and what a good trade he had made in exchanging a dying cow for a sack full of victuals. On hearing this fine story, his wife began to snarl. He begged her to keep her ill-humor to herself, and to hang on her biggest pot. "You will see what I have brought," said he. "Wait a little, and you will thank me." He opened the sack, when out stepped a little man, all in gray, like a mouse.

"How are you, good people ?" said he, with the air of a prince. "I hope that, instead of cooking me, you will give me something to eat ; this little journey has made me very hungry."

The peasant dropped upon his bench as if he were thunderstruck.

"There !" said his wife ; "I was sure it would turn out so. Here is a new piece of folly. But what else can one expect of a husband ? Here you have lost the cow, that was our only means of livelihood, and, now that we have nothing, you bring us another mouth to feed. I wish you had stayed in the snow with your sack and its treasure."

The good woman would have gone on talking till dooms-
day, if the little gray man had not thrice remonstrated with
her that hard words would not fill the pot, and that the wisest course was to go and hunt for game.   He went out at
once, in spite of the darkness, wind, and snow, and soon
came back, bringing a fat sheep.

"There!" said he; "kill this creature, and do not let us
die of starvation."

The old peasant and his wife looked askance at the little
man and his booty.   This boon, that fell, as it were, from
the clouds, savored strongly of theft ; but, when hunger cries
aloud, farewell to scruples.   Lawful prey or not, the sheep
was hungrily eaten.

From that day plenty reigned in the peasant's household.
One sheep followed another, and the honest man, more

credulous than ever, marvelled within himself whether he had not gained by the exchange, when, instead of the hundred cows that he expected, heaven had sent him so skilful a purveyor as the little gray man.

There are two sides to everything. While the sheep multiplied in the old man's house they perceptibly diminished in the royal flock which was at pasture in the neighborhood. The head shepherd, in great distress, informed the king that for some time, in spite of his redoubled vigilance, the finest wethers in the flock had disappeared one after another. Some adroit thief had certainly taken up his abode in the neighborhood. It did not take long to discover that there was a stranger in the peasant's cabin, whom no one knew, and who had come from none knew whither. The king ordered the stranger to be instantly brought before him. The little gray man set out without a frown, but the peasant and his wife began to feel a little remorse on thinking that receivers and thieves were hung on the same gallows.

When the little gray man appeared at court, the king asked him whether, by chance, he had not heard that five fat sheep had been stolen from the royal flock.

"Yes, your majesty!" answered the little man; "it was I that took them."

"By what right?" said the prince.

"Your majesty, I took them because an old man and his wife were suffering with hunger, while you, oh, king, were rolling in wealth, and could not use one tenth of your income. It seemed to me just that these honest people should live on your superfluity, rather than die of want, while you knew not what to do with your abundance."

The king stood stupefied at such audacity; then, looking the little man in a manner that boded no good, "As far as I can see," said he, "your chief talent is stealing."

The little man bowed with modest pride.

"Very well!" said the king; "you deserve to be hung; but I forgive you, on condition that, by this time to-morrow, you shall have stolen from my shepherds my black bull, which they tell me they guard so carefully."

"Your majesty, you ask an impossibility. How do you expect me to deceive such vigilance?"

"If you do not do it," returned the king, "you will be hung," and with a gesture he dismissed the thief, while all around echoed, "Hung!" "hung!" "hung!"

The little gray man returned to the hut, where he was tenderly received by the peasant and his wife. He only told them, however, that he needed a rope, and that he should leave the next morning at daybreak. They gave him the cow's old halter, upon which he went to bed and slept soundly.

At the first dawn of day the little gray man set out with his rope. He went into the forest along the road by which the king's shepherds were to pass, and, choosing a great oak, well in sight, hung himself by the neck to its largest bough. He took good care, however, not to make a slip-noose.

Two shepherds soon came by, leading the black bull.

"Look," said one, "the knave has already got his reward. It is certain, at least, that he did not steal his halter. Good-bye, my fine fellow! There is no danger of your taking the king's bull."

No sooner were the shepherds out of sight than the little gray man sprang down from the tree, ran up a cross-road, and hung himself anew to a great oak near the road. The shepherds were astonished to see another man hung.

"Who is that?" cried one. "Do I see double? Here is the man that was hung over yonder."

" ' Why, here is the man that was hung over yonder!' "

"How stupid you are!" said his companion; "how can a man be hung in two places at once? This is another robber, that is all."

"I tell you that it is the same one," returned the first shepherd; "I know him by his coat and his grimace."

"And I will bet that it is some one else," said the second shepherd, who was strong-minded.

The bet was taken, and the two shepherds tied the bull to a tree, and ran back to the first oak. But no sooner were they out of sight than the little gray man leaped from his gibbet, and stealthily led the bull to the peasant's cottage. He was joyfully welcomed, and the animal was put into the stable till it could be sold.

The two shepherds returned at night to the castle with hanging heads and dejected air. The king saw at once that a trick had been played them. He sent for the little gray man, who presented himself with the serenity of a hero.

"You have stolen my bull," said the king.

"Your majesty," answered the little man, "I only did it in obedience to your commands."

"Very well!" said the king; "here are ten gold crowns as its ransom; but if, in two days, you do not steal the clothes off my bed while I am asleep, I will hang you."

"Your majesty, do not ask such a thing. You are too well guarded for a poor man like me to be able even to approach the castle."

"If you do not do it," said the king, "I shall have the pleasure of hanging you."

When evening came, the little gray man, who had returned to the hut, took a long rope and a basket. This basket he lined with moss, and put in it a cat that had just kittened, with all her litter. Then, groping his way through the thick darkness, he slipped into the castle, and mounted to the roof without being seen. To enter the garret, saw through a plank of the floor, and let himself down through this opening into the king's chamber, was the work of a few moments. Once there, he carefully turned down the bedclothes, and laid the cat and kittens in the royal

bed. He then clambered up the bedpost, and seated himself on the canopy, and in this elevated position waited to see what would happen.

The palace clock struck eleven, and the

king and queen entered their apartment. Having un-
dressed, both knelt down and said their prayers; after
which the king put out the light, and the queen got into
bed. All at once she shrieked, and sprang to the middle
of the room.

"Are you mad?" said the king. "Do you want to alarm
the whole castle?"

"My dear," answered she, "come away from that bed, I
beg of you; I felt a burning breath there, and my feet
touched something hairy."

"Why not say at once that the devil is in the bed?" said
the king, laughing contemptuously. "All women have the
heart of a hare and the head of a linnet."

Upon which, like a true hero, he bravely lay down under
the coverlet, and instantly sprang out, dragging after him
the cat, which had fastened its claws into his thigh. At
the king's shrieks the sentinel rushed to the door, and knocked
thrice with his halberd, as a signal that aid was at hand.

"Silence!" said the prince, ashamed of his weakness, and
not wishing to be caught in a fright.

He struck a match, lighted the lamp, and saw in the bed
the cat, tenderly licking her kittens.

"This is too much!" he cried. "This impudent creature
has no respect for our crown, but takes our royal couch in
which to deposit her litter. Wait, puss, and I will give you
what you deserve."

"She will bite you," said the queen; "she may be mad."

"Don't be afraid, my dear!" returned the good prince,
and, raising the corners of the under-sheet, he wrapped the
whole litter in it; after which he rolled it in the coverlet
and upper-sheet, made a huge bundle of the whole, and threw
it out of the window.

"Now," said he to the queen, "let us go to your room,

and sleep in peace, since we are avenged."

The king slept, and pleasant dreams lulled his slumbers; but while he reposed, a man climbed on the roof, and fastened a rope thereto, by which he let himself down to the ground. Once there, he groped for the bundle, took it on his back, leaped over the wall, and ran off through the snow. The sentinels declared the next morning that a phantom had flitted before them, and that they had heard the cries of a new-born child.

When he awoke the next morning, the king collected his thoughts, and began for the first time to reflect calmly. He suspected that he had been the victim of some trickery, and that the author of the crime was the little gray man. He sent for him at once.

The little gray man came, carrying on his shoulder the clothes, freshly ironed. He bent his knee before the queen, and said, in a respectful tone,

"Your majesty knows that what I did was only in obedience to the king's orders. I hope that you will be good enough to forgive me."

"Very well," said the queen; "but never do it again, or you will kill me with fright."

"But I do not forgive you," said the king, greatly vexed
that the queen should take it upon herself to show clemency
without consulting her lord and master. "Listen to me,
you scoundrel. If by to-morrow night you have not stolen
the queen herself from her castle, to-morrow night you shall
be hung."

"Your majesty!" cried the little man, "hang me at once,
and spare me twenty-four hours of anguish. How do you
expect me to succeed in such an undertaking? It would be
easier to pull down the moon with my teeth."

"That is your business and not mine," returned the king.
"Meanwhile, I shall order the gallows to be set up."

The little man went out in despair. He buried his face
in his hands, and sobbed ready to break his heart. The
king laughed for the first time.

Towards dusk a holy Capuchin monk, with his rosary in

his hand, and his wallet upon his back, came to the castle, according to custom, to beg for his convent. When the queen gave him alms,

"Madam!" said he, "God will reward your charity. Even now I bring you a recompense. To-morrow, as you well know, a wretch, who is doubtless guilty, is to be hung in the castle."

"Alas!" returned the queen, "I forgave him heartily, and would gladly have saved his life."

"That cannot be," said the monk; "but this man, who is a kind of wizard, may make you a valuable gift before he dies. I know that he possesses three mar-

vellous secrets, one alone of which is worth a kingdom. One of these he may be ready to bequeath to her who looked on him with pity."

"What are these secrets?" asked the queen.

"By virtue of the first, a woman can make her husband do whatever she chooses."

"Ah!" said the princess, shrugging her shoulders, "there is nothing wonderful about that recipe. From the time of Eve, of blessed memory, this mystery has been handed down from mother to daughter. What is the second secret?"

"The second one confers wisdom and goodness on its possessor."

"Indeed!" said the queen, in an absent-minded way; "and the third?"

"The third secures to the woman who possesses it unequalled beauty, and the power of pleasing to the end of her life."

"Father, that is the secret that I want!" cried the queen.

"Nothing is easier than to obtain it," said the monk. "It is only necessary that before dying, and while he is still at full liberty, the wizard should take both your hands, and blow three times upon your hair."

"Let him come!" said the queen. "Father, go bring him here!"

"That cannot be," said the monk. "The king has given the strictest orders that this man shall not enter the castle. If he sets his foot within these grounds, he dies on the spot. Do not deprive him of the few hours he has to live."

"But, father, the king has forbidden me to go out till to-morrow evening."

"That is a pity," said the monk. "I see that you must give up this priceless treasure. It would be sweet, however, never to grow old, but always to remain young and beautiful, and, above all, beloved."

"Alas! father, you are quite right. The king's command is the height of injustice. But even if I should attempt to go, the guards would stop me. Don't look so astonished; you see how the king treats me, with his caprices. I am the most unhappy of women."

"My heart is wrung," said the monk. "What tyranny! What barbarism! Well, madam, you should not give way to such unreasonable commands. It is your duty to do as you please."

"But how can I do so?"

"There is one way, if you are strong in the consciousness that you are right. Get into this sack, and I will carry you out of the castle at the risk of my life. And fifty years hence, when you are as young and beautiful as you are to-day, you will applaud yourself for resisting the will of a ty-rant."

"Very well," said the queen. "But is not this some snare laid for me?"

"Madam," said the holy man, raising his hands to heaven and beating his breast, "as sure as I am a monk, you have nothing to fear. Besides, I will stay by your side all the time you are with this unhappy man."

"And you will bring me back to the castle?"

"I swear it."

"And with the secret?"

"With the secret. But if your majesty has any scruples, stay here and let the secret die with its possessor, unless he chooses to give it to some more confiding woman."

For her sole answer, the queen crept into the sack ; the monk drew the strings together, threw the bundle over his shoulder, and crossed the courtyard with measured steps. On his way he met the king, who was making his rounds.

"The alms must have been plentiful to-day, judging by appearances," said the king.

"Sire," answered the monk, "your majesty's charity is inexhaustible, and I fear that I have abused it. Perhaps I had better leave this sack and its contents."

"No! no!" said the king; "carry it away, father, and good riddance to it. I fancy that all you have there is not worth much. You will make a slender supper."

"I wish your majesty may sup with as good an appetite," returned the monk, as he went away, muttering under his breath.

The supper-bell rang, and the king entered the dining-room, rubbing his hands. He was satisfied with himself, and he hoped to have vengeance—a double reason for being hungry.

"The queen not down yet!" said he, sarcastically. "That does not surprise me, however; unpunctuality is the virtue of women."

He was about to sit down to the table, when three soldiers entered, crossing their halberds, and driving before them the little gray man.

"Sire," said one of the guards, "this fellow has had the audacity to enter the courtyard of the castle in spite of the royal command. We should have hung him on the spot, without disturbing your majesty's supper, but he pretends that he has a message from the queen, and that he is the bearer of a state secret."

"The queen!" cried the king, amazed. "Where is she, wretch? and what have you done with her?"

"I have stolen her," said the little man, coolly.

"But how?" asked the king.

"Sire, that monk, with the huge sack on his back, to whom your majesty deigned to say, 'Take it away, and good riddance to it'"—

"Was you!" said the prince. "Wretch, there is no longer

any safety for me. One of these days you will take me, and my kingdom into the bargain."

"Sire, I come to ask you for more than that."

"You frighten me," said the king. "Who are you — a wizard, or the devil in person?"

"No, sire. I am simply the Prince of Holar. You have a marriageable daughter. I was on my way to ask her hand, when the bad weather forced me and my squire to take refuge with the curate of Skalholt. There I chanced to fall in with a foolish countryman, who made me play the part you know. All that I have done, moreover, has been only to obey and please your majesty."

"All right," said the king. "I understand ; or, rather, I don't understand. No matter. Prince Holar, I would rather have you for a son-in-law than a neighbor. Where is the queen?"

"Sire, she is here. My squire was ordered to bring her to the palace."

The queen soon entered, a little abashed at her credulity, but easily consoled by thinking that she would have so clever a son-in-law.

"But the famous secret," she whispered to the Prince of Holar ; "you owe it to me."

"The secret of being always beautiful," said the prince, "is to be always beloved."

"And the way to be always beloved?" said the queen.

"Is to be good and simple, and to do your husband's will."

"He dares say that he is a wizard," said the queen, indignantly raising her hands to heaven.

"Have done with these mysteries !" cried the king, who was beginning to be nervous. "Prince Holar, when you marry our daughter, you will have more time than you

will want to talk with your mother-in-law. The supper is
cooling. To table! Amuse yourself, my son-in-law! Give
the evening to pleasure! To-morrow you will be married."

At these words, which he thought witty, the king looked
at the queen, who answered with such a frown that he instantly began to rub his chin, and watch the flies on the
ceiling.

Here end the adventures of Prince Holar. Happy days
have no history. We know, however, that he succeeded his
father-in-law, and that he was a great king. Something of a
liar and something of a robber; bold and cunning, he had
the virtues of a conqueror. He took from his neighbors
more than a thousand leagues of snow, which he lost and
won three times by the sacrifice of half a dozen armies.
His name, however, figures gloriously in the celebrated annals of Skalholt and Holar, and to these famous documents
we refer our reader.

GAGLIUSO; OR, THE GOOD CAT.

A FAIRY TALE FROM THE PENTAMERON.

INGRATITUDE, sirs, is a nail that blights the tree of courtesy when once it is driven in it; it is a broken arch, that lays in ruins the foundations of affection; it is a handful of soot that, falling into the dish of friendship, destroys its taste and flavor, as is seen and proved daily, as well as by the tale which I am about to tell.

There was once in my beloved city of Naples a poor old man named Gagliuso, so squalid and destitute that he was as naked as a worm. Feeling himself at the point of death, he said to his two children, Oratiello and Pippo, "My sons, I am summoned to pay the debt of nature. Believe me, Christians as you are, that my only regret in quitting this sad abode of toil and pain is that I leave you without a farthing. Alas! you will have less than a fly could carry off on his foot. I have led a dog's life; I have dined off an empty stomach, and gone to bed in the dark. But in spite of all, I wish on my deathbed to leave you some token of my love. Oratiello, my first-born, take that wallet hanging on the wall, and may you find in it every night what I have often sought in vain all day, a crust of bread. As to you, my youngest, take the cat. My children, remember your dear father." With these words, he burst into tears, and a little while after said, "Farewell, it is night."

Oratiello buried his father at the public expense; after which he plucked up his courage, and went down to the bay to help the fishermen draw the seine.

But Pippo, looking at the cat, cried, "See what a fine legacy my father has left me! I cannot keep myself, and here I have two mouths to feed!"

The cat heard these lamentations, and remarked, "You complain without cause, and have more luck than sense. You do not know your good-fortune, for I can make you rich if I set about it."

Pippo felt that she was right. He stroked the cat three or four times, and warmly besought the favor of Dame Puss, who took compassion on the poor lad. She went out every morning, to the bay, or the fish-market, where she managed to lay hold of some huge mullet or superb sword-fish, which she carried to the king, saying, "Your majesty's slave, Signor

DESSINE PAR H PILLE   EAU-FORTE DE P. HANESSE

"She managed to lay hold of some huge mullet or superb sword-fish,
which she carried to the king."

Gagliuso, sends this fish, with his compliments, as a small gift to a great prince."

Upon which the king, with the pleased air of one receiving a present, would answer, "Tell this stranger gentleman that I am infinitely obliged to him."

Another time the cat would scour the fields and marshes, and when the hunters shot down a blackbird, lark, or woodcock, would snatch up the game, and hurry with it on the same errand to the king. She used this artifice so long that at last, one morning, the king said, "I am under so many obligations to Signor Gagliuso, that I should like to make his acquaintance and thank him for all his courtesy." The cat replied, "Signor Gagliuso's blood and life are at your majesty's disposal. My master will wait upon you to-morrow morning without fail."

Morning having come, the cat hastened to the king, crying, "Signor Gagliuso begs you to excuse him for not presenting himself before you. Some of his rascally valets ran off with his clothes last night ; the thieves have not left him a shirt to his back."

On hearing this, the king ordered a quantity of linen and wearing apparel to be taken from his own wardrobe and sent to Gagliuso. Before two hours had passed our hero entered the palace, escorted by the cat. The king received him most graciously, and seating him by his side, ordered a magnificent feast to be served him.

While they were at dinner, Gagliuso turned from time to time to the cat, and said, "Look here, Puss, keep an eye

on our things!" to which she answered, "Hush! hush! don't
speak of such trifles." The king asked what troubled Gagliuso, whereupon the cat said that he would like a small
lemon, when the king sent to the garden for a whole basketful.
But Gagliuso continued to repeat the same thing, while the
cat tried to hush him, and when the king insisted upon knowing what was the matter, invented one excuse after another
to conceal her master's meanness, in thinking that any one
there would be likely to steal his hat and cloak.

At last, after sitting long at the table, talking of one thing
and another, Gagliuso asked permission to withdraw. Left
alone with the king, the cat extolled her master's merit, wit,
and good sense, and, above all, the immense wealth that

he possessed in the Roman Campagna and Lombardy. He was just such a son-in-law as a crowned head might desire. The king, asking what his fortune might be, the cat declared that it was impossible to reckon the value of the goods and chattels of this Crœsus, who did not know himself what he was worth. But if the king wished to be sure, it was a very easy matter; he had only to send some trusty messengers across the frontier, and they would learn for themselves that there was no wealth in the world like Gagliuso's.

The king summoned his faithful counsellors, and ordered them carefully to inquire into the affair. They followed the cat, who, as soon as they had crossed the frontier, ran on before, on the pretence of preparing refreshments. Wherever she found a flock of sheep, cows, horses, or swine, she said to the shepherds, or keepers, "Look here! there is a company of robbers coming to plunder everything they find. If you wish to escape and save your property, you must say, 'All this belongs to Signor Gagliuso!' and they will not touch a hair."

She repeated the same thing at all the farms along the way, so that, wherever the king's messengers went, they heard the same song. All that they saw belonged to Signor Gagliuso. Tired of asking the same question, they returned to the king and told him wonders concerning Signor Gagliuso's possessions. On hearing this the monarch promised the cat a heavy fee if she would make the match, and her friendly tongue bobbed back and forth like a shuttle till it had woven the whole intrigue. Gagliuso offered himself, and the king gave him a fat dowry with his daughter.

After a month's merry-making Gagliuso told his royal father-in-law that he wished to carry his bride to his estates. The king accompanied them as far as the frontier, after which they went to Lombardy, where, by the cat's advice, Gagliuso bought a vast domain with the title of baron.

Master Gagliuso, on seeing himself as rich as a prince, thanked the cat in the warmest way imaginable, telling her over and over again that it was to her that he owed his wealth and grandeur. The wit of a cat had done more for him than all his father's sense. She might dispose of the property and life of her dear master as she saw fit. And when she died—would to Heaven that she might live a hundred years!—he pledged her his word that he would have her embalmed and put in a golden casket, which he would keep in his chamber, that he might always have her cherished remembrance before his eyes.

The cat was greatly puffed up with all these fine speeches. Before three days had passed, she stretched herself at full length along the garden terrace, pretending to be dead.

"Husband! husband!" cried Gagliuso's wife, "what a great misfortune! the cat is dead!"

"The deuce take her," answered Gagliuso; "better that she should die than we."

"What shall we do with her?" asked the princess.

"Take her by the paw and fling her out of the window."

On hearing this funeral oration, which was not exactly what she was looking for, the cat jumped up, and cried: "So these are your thanks to me for cleansing you of your filth! This is your gratitude for stripping you of rags fit for nothing but a wad for a distaff! This is the way you reward me for feeding you, you scoundrel! for clothing you, you wretch! But it is wasting soap to wash an ass's head. Accursed be all I have done for you. You are not even worth the trouble of spitting in your face. A fine gold casket you have made ready for me! A splendid funeral you have ordered for me! Well, puss, you have sweated, labored, and worn yourself out, to be paid in such coin! Fool that you were, not to know that service is no inheritance. The philosopher was right who said, 'He who goes to bed an ass will get up an ass.' The more one does, the more one may do. But fine words and foul deeds deceive wise men and fools alike."

With these words she started for the door. Gagliuso followed, and attempted in the humblest accents to soften her. His labor was in vain; she would not return, but went straight onward, without turning her head, saying, "Beware of enriching a pauper, he is sure to turn out a villain."

And now, friendly reader, that you know Basilio's version of Puss in Boots, referred to in our Preface, as well as the old, familiar one, tell us which is the original and which the copy. Guess if you can, and choose if you dare.

A learned friend suggests that it is not necessary that one of these stories should be a repetition of the other ; both may have come from a common theme. It is a melody which has been sung in many countries, but though it has produced more than one variation in its journeyings, it is still the same melody, which each nurse sings in her own key.

Here is another example ; a Middle Age fable, found in the Recitals of a Minstrel of Rheims of the 13th Century, published by the Historical Society of France. We give it as it was chanted by a minstrel in the days of St. Louis.

THE WOLF AND THE GOAT.

A MEDIÆVAL FABLE.

THERE was once a wolf named Isengrin, who had a piece of arable land. He went to a goat, with two kids, and said to her, "Dame Goat, I have a bit of an old vineyard that I would like to have you farm for me on shares. The soil is so fertile that it will bear wheat without enriching; and, I assure you, that I would much rather till it all myself than divide it with others. But I have an important suit before my noble lord Lion, against Belin, the shepherd, who pretends that I have eaten two of his sheep, so that I have to go to court every week, and furnish counsel, at a heavy cost."

"I dare not," answered the goat.

"Why not?"

"Forsooth, because you are a great and mighty lord, with powerful connections, while I am an humble and defenceless creature. It would be useless for me ever to bring a suit against you, in case we should disagree."

"Zounds!" cried the wolf, "Dame Goat, my fair friend, what have you to fear from me? I swear by the faith I owe Dame Hersent, my wife, and by the twelve living children she has given me, that I will deal honestly by you, and never wrong you in all my life."

"Well," said the goat, "I will do it; but I have great misgivings that you will not give me my fair share."

The wolf went away. The goat cleared the ground of the vine-roots, ploughed it, and sowed it with wheat, which yielded a fine crop. When harvest-time had come, she went to the wolf and said, "Sir Wolf, our wheat is ripe; will you come, or send some one, to look after it?"

"In faith," returned the wolf, "I can neither go nor send; gather it in yourself; put the grain on one side and the straw on the other, and when I return from court we will make a fair division."

The goat left, unable to obtain any other answer. She cut and thrashed the wheat, and put the grain on one side and the straw on the other.

No sooner had she finished than the wolf appeared. This was what he had been waiting for. He went to the goat, and said, loftily, "Come, dame, shall we divide the crop?"

"Whenever you please, noble sir," answered she. "Here is the grain on one side, and the straw on the other, as you commanded; take half of each."

"Out upon you, foolish beast, you do not know what you are talking about. I shall do no such thing."

"What will you do, then?" asked the goat.

"Forsooth, I am a great lord, and have an expensive household to keep up. My needs are greater than yours, you underling. A little will suffice for you; you shall have the straw and I will take the grain."

"Oh, my lord, you are unjust; for God's sake, take your share and leave me mine."

"Zounds!" cried the wolf, "I shall do nothing of the kind. And I warn you that I shall come back to-morrow to know whether you will do as I wish."

The wolf departed. The goat stood aghast. Suddenly,

she bethought herself of two mastiffs that she had nursed, and that lived near by, at the Abbey of Citeaux. One was named Tabarel and the other Roenel. The goat went straightway there, and found them sitting by the gate. On seeing their foster-mother they ran to meet her, gave her a warm welcome, and asked what brought her hither. She told them how the wolf wished to treat her.

"In faith," cried both the dogs, "by our fangs, but this shall not be. Return home, dear mother, we promise to be there early in the morning, to see the division between you and Isengrin. Please Heaven, Sir Wolf shall not wrong you while we are by!"

The goat returned home, and found her kids crying. She quieted them, and went to bed. However, she slept little, and rose very early, praying to God for aid.

The two brothers, Tabarel and Roenel, appeared. They bade her good-morning, and asked if Isengrin had come.

"Not yet," she answered.

"Mother," said the dogs, "we have thought of a good plan. We will creep under this heap of straw, and curl ourselves up there until we see and hear what Isengrin means to do. For, if he knew we were here, perhaps he would not come, but would wait until we were gone."

"You are right, my children," replied the goat. And the dogs crept under the straw.

Isengrin soon appeared, bringing with him his friend and counsellor, Reynard the fox, who had played him more than one scurvy trick. "Well, dame," said he to the goat, "have you consulted your friends yet?"

"Whom could I consult?" answered the goat. "Take your share, and leave me mine."

"Grumble as much as you like, it shall be as I say," exclaimed the wolf.

While the wolf and goat were disputing, Reynard cast his eyes on the heap of straw and saw the dogs' tails sticking out.

"Neighbor, be on your guard," said he to Isengrin. "I see more in this business than you do."

"Come what will, Sir Reynard, I mean to have my way in the matter. I will have the grain and she shall take the straw."

" Reynard cast his eyes on the heap of straw and saw the dogs' tails
sticking out."

10*

"Mark me, neighbor," said Reynard, "what I tell you is only for your good; and may good befall you! Beware! I am going away."

Reynard quitted Isengrin and mounted a hillock close by to see how the affair would end. Isengrin and his cartmen took their sacks and filled them with wheat.

"Holy Mother, help me!" cried the goat. "My children," she called to Roenel and Tabarel, "you see how I am treated!" And, behold, the dogs sprang from the straw, and, without stopping to argue the matter, fell upon the wolf, threw him down, seized him by the throat, and inflicted more than a hundred wounds upon his body, so that locks of hair flew in all directions. They worried him until his pulse and breath were gone, and left him for dead.

Then they took the wheat; and while they were carrying

it to the granary of the goat, the cartmen hastened, with great difficulty, to lift Isengrin into the cart, and drove home with him at full speed.

And, behold, Reynard came to meet them. He had seen the whole affair, and chuckled over it, for such was his nature. The pain of others was his delight. He approached the mangled wolf, and said, in a honeyed tone:

"Good neighbor, I am grieved at your accident. If you had listened to me it would not have happened. I told you to be on your guard, for I saw more in the business than you did."

"Reynard, Reynard!" exclaimed the wolf, "he who has no friend but you has none at all. I have been put to shame; but I will have my revenge." And he turned his back on Reynard, who made a face at him.

Isengrin was carried to his house, where Dame Hersent, his wife, and his children were looking for him. When they saw him stretched in the cart on a wisp of hay, they began to laugh at him, saying, "He who tackles a goat will get a butting. Is this the grain you were to bring us for our wheat cakes?" Such was the greeting which Isengrin received from his household. Whence came the saying, "When a man falls the whole world treads upon him." He was lifted from the cart, groaning and shamefaced, and carried to bed. It was five months before his wounds were healed.

Let us return to Roenel and Tabarel. When they had carried the wheat to the granary, they said to the goat, "Good mother, we are going to the abbey, which is close by; if you need us we shall be ready to help you. Take this horn and blow on it in case of danger, when we will run to your aid."

"Many thanks, dear children," answered the goat.

"He who tackles a goat will get a butting."

"Blessed be the day I nursed you." The dogs bade her farewell, and returned home.

As soon as he had somewhat recovered from his adventure Isengrin went to see the goat, but she was on her guard, and as soon as she spied him began to blow the horn. And, lo! sounds of *Bow, wow, wow!* were heard in the distance, as if to say, *Here we are! here we are!* Upon this, Master Wolf pricked up his ears directly, and began to amble gently along, then took to his heels, with his tail between his legs, as if the devil were after him. He never came back again.

Violence and Knavery almost always end in the ruin of the author. Honesty is the best policy.

This mediæval fable is a new version of the Wolf and the Lamb. But the wolf has had the upper hand long enough, and here the lamb, or, in other words, the goat, has its turn. It is a law of nature for us to turn things wrong side out after using them on the right side. In this way David overthrows Goliath, Omphale makes Hercules hold her distaff, and Delilah robs Samson of his strength. Nothing is more natural. It is the swinging of the pendulum ; or what the universities call the law of compensation. For example, if our philosophers are to be believed, man is descended from the ape. This will hold true until a new order of things prevails, when it will be found that the ape is descended from man. It is inevitable.

THE WICKED DAUGHTERS-IN-LAW.

ONCE upon a time there were three old women, who were neighbors, and who lived together in the greatest harmony. Each of them had a son. The three young men, who were brought up together and were in the same business, loved each other like brothers. The friendship of the children rendered the mutual affection of the mothers even warmer than ever. But the good women were wise; they reflected that death was approaching, and that when they were gone their sons would be left alone. Their great desire was, therefore, to see them marry.

One day, as the three friends were walking together, they saw three young girls in a balcony, who seemed to them so charming that they asked them in marriage that very evening. They did not have to wait long for an answer, and the three

marriages took place the next day. Then, as they were very fond of each other, and were not rich, it was agreed that they should all live together under one roof, and that the poor mothers should pass their old age peacefully with their children.

Business compelled the three young merchants to travel,

and it once chanced that they were all three obliged to be
absent for some time.   They were scarcely on the road when
their wives began to quarrel with their mothers-in-law.   To
live with these old women was unendurable; and they were
determined at any cost to rid themselves of this burden.
Two of them proposed simply to choke their mothers-in-law,
but the youngest objected.   "No," said she, "that would be
cruel, and, besides, it would be no revenge; it is better to
torment them from morning till night, and from night till
morning."

No sooner said than done.   One of the wives sent her
mother-in-law to school, to learn to read and write.   It was
a little late, at seventy!   The second one sent her mother-
in-law to a fiddler, to learn to play the fiddle; and the third
shut hers up in the cellar, with a basket of eggs to hatch.   In
this way the fair dames rid themselves of their troublesome
companions, and led a merry and contented life in their husbands' absence.

On returning to town, the three friends were astonished at the uproar that prevailed in the school. They looked through the window, and saw an old woman trying to say the alphabet. As she did not know the letters, the teacher scolded and punished her, to the great amusement of the mischievous urchins.

" Is not that your mother?" asked one of the friends of his companion.

" Ho! there ; mother, what are you doing at school?" cried the young man.

" It was your wife, my daughter-in-law, that sent me here. You see how I am treated."

" Be patient for a little while, mother, I will soon come and take you away."

Two paces beyond lived the fiddler, and it was almost as noisy there as at the school. A poor old woman was squeaking her bow in such a fashion as to set all the dogs in the neighborhood howling, while all around scoffed at her, and roared with laughter.

" Oh, mother!" cried one of the friends, "what are you doing there?"

" Alas, my son, it was your wife, my daughter-in-law, that set me to learn this trade."

" Be patient for a little while, mother, I will soon come and take you away."

On approaching the house, they heard groans in the cellar. The three companions looked through the darkness, and discerned an old woman crouching over a basket, with nothing near her but a crust of dry bread and a jug of water.

" Ah! mother," cried one of the friends, "what are you doing there?"

" Alas! my son, it was your wife, my daughter-in-law, who put me where you find me."

"Be patient for a little while, mother, I will soon come and take you away."

The three friends entered the house, their hearts burning with wrath. They found their wives dressed in mourning, with tears in their eyes.

"What has happened?"

"Alas!" cried each of the wives, "I have lost my dear mother-in-law."

"What! all three dead?"

"Yes," answered their wives, "all three are gone."

The three husbands sighed, and seemed deeply grieved, like good sons. But the very next morning they said to their wives,

"Dress yourselves handsomely, and we will take a sail and enjoy ourselves."

The delighted wives put on their best gowns. How happy

they were to have rid themselves of their mothers-in-law, and so easily deceived their husbands. They would have laughed less had they known of three sacks in the boat, hidden under a seat.

As soon as they were out at sea, the faces of the three men turned black as thunder. Each of them seized his wife, thrust her into a sack, and flung her into the water, crying, "Go send your mother-in-law to school, to play the fiddle, or to hatch eggs!"

After which the three sons took their mothers home with them, and vowed never to marry again.

THE SPINNING QUEEN.

A DALMATIAN FAIRY TALE.

THERE was once a Dalmatian woman who had a daughter as beautiful as the day, but hopelessly lazy and unwilling to do any kind of work. After vainly trying to coax her to be useful, the mother took her to the forest, near a crossroad, and began to beat her with all her might. Just then the prince chanced to pass that way, who asked why she treated the girl so cruelly.

"My lord," said she, "it is because our daughter wears our life out with her intolerable industry. She spins up everything, even to the moss that grows on the walls."

"Let me have her," said the prince. "I will give her wherewith to spin to her heart's content."

"Take her," said the mother, "take her, I am glad to be rid of her."

The prince carried her home, enchanted with such a valuable acquisition. The same evening, he shut the young girl up alone in a chamber with a huge load of flax. What to do in such a plight she knew not. She paced up and down, wringing her hands, and crying, "What will become of me? I can't spin, and I won't spin."

Her anguish was at its height, when behold, at midnight, three old witches tapped at the window-pane, and she quickly let them in.

"On seeing how ugly they were, the prince could not forbear saying to his bride 'Your aunts are not handsome.'"

"If you will ask us to your wedding, we will help you spin this evening," said they.

"Spin, ladies," she answered; "I will ask you with all my heart."

And behold, the three witches spun and spun all the flax that was there while Miss Lazybones slept at her ease.

In the morning, when the prince came to the chamber, he saw the whole wall hung with skeins of thread and the girl asleep. He went out on tiptoe, and forbade any one to enter the room, so that the spinner could rest after her hard labor. This did not prevent him from sending thither on the same day a second huge load of flax. The witches returned at midnight, and finished the work, as the night before. The prince was wonder-struck; and as there was nothing more to spin in the house, he said to the young girl,

"I will marry you, for you are the Spinning Queen."

On the evening before the wedding, the pretended spinner said to the prince, "I must invite my aunts."

"They shall be welcome," was his answer.

Once admitted, the three witches grouped themselves around the stove. They were hideous to behold. On seeing how ugly they were, the prince could not forbear saying to his bride, "Your aunts are not handsome."

Then, approaching the first witch, he asked her why her nose was so long.

"My dear nephew," she answered, "it is through spinning so much. When one spins all the time and wags her head all day long, the nose grows long insensibly."

The prince passed on to the second, and asked her why her lips were so thick.

"My dear nephew," said she, "it is through spinning so much. When one spins all the time, and moistens the thread all day long, the lips grow thick insensibly."

He then asked the third why she was so humpbacked.

"My dear nephew," said she, "it is through spinning so much. When one sits bent over her work all day long, the back becomes humped insensibly."

Upon this, the prince was seized with such a fear that, through spinning, his wife might become as horrible as these three frights, that he flung both spindle and distaff into the fire, and forbade her ever again to spin a thread, under penalty of his deep displeasure. What anger this caused the bride, I leave those to guess who resemble her.

THE KING OF THE SERPENTS.

A FAIRY TALE OF THE DANUBE.

THERE was once a shepherd who had served his master zealously and faithfully for long years. One day, as he was watching his flocks, he heard a hissing noise, that came from the woods. Wishing to learn what it was, he entered the forest and followed the sound. After going on a little way, he saw that the dry grass and dead leaves had caught fire, making a blazing circle, in the midst of which a serpent was hissing. The shepherd stopped to see what it would do, as the flames were fast closing in upon it. On spying him, the serpent cried, "For God's sake, save me from the fire!" The shepherd stretched his crook over the flames to the snake, which twined around it, and glided on to his hand and thence to his throat, around which it coiled itself like a necklace.

"Alas!" cried the frightened shepherd, "have I saved you only for my own destruction?"

"Fear nothing," answered the snake, "but take me back to my father, the King of the Serpents."

The shepherd tried to excuse himself, saying that he could not leave his flock without a keeper; but the serpent cried

" Do not trouble yourself about your sheep; no harm will
come to them; only make haste as fast as you can."

The shepherd ran through the forest with the snake coiled
around his neck till he reached a gate made of adders inter-
laced together. The snake gave a hiss, upon which the adders separated, and made way for them to pass. The serpent then said to the shepherd, "When we reach the castle,
my father will offer you anything you wish: silver, gold,
jewels, and all the most precious treasures of earth; accept

none of them, but only ask to know the language of the animals. He will long refuse this favor, but will grant it at last." While talking they reached the castle, and were met by the King of the Serpents, who exclaimed, with tears in his eyes, " My child, where have you been ?"

The young serpent told his father how he had been surrounded by fire and had been saved by the shepherd. The King of the Serpents then turned to the shepherd and said,

" What shall I give you for saving my child ?"

" Teach me the language of the animals," he answered, " that I may talk with all the earth as you do."

" That would be of no use to you," said the king, " for if I should enable you to understand this language, and you should tell any one, you would die on the spot. Ask me for something that will serve you better, and it shall be yours."

" If you wish to pay me," returned the shepherd, " teach me the language of the animals ; if not, adieu, and God be with you ! I want nothing else."

He feigned to depart. The king called him back, saying, " Stop ! come here, since you insist upon it. Open your mouth."

The shepherd did as he was bid; the king blew into his mouth, and said, " Now blow in turn in mine." When they had blown thus three times into each other's mouths, the king said, " Now you understand the language of the animals. God be with you ; but if you care for life, beware of betraying the secret, for if you say a word of it to any one, you are a dead man."

The shepherd returned. As he passed through the wood he heard what the birds, the insects, and all on the earth were saying. On reaching his flock, he found it safe and in good order, and stretched himself on the ground for a

nap. Scarcely had he lain down when two crows perched
on the bough of a tree overhead, and said, in their own language, "What if this shepherd knew that just under the

spot where that black lamb is standing there is a cavern
full of gold and silver!"

No sooner had the shepherd heard this than he went and

told his master. They brought a wagon, and dug until they found the door of the cavern, the treasure of which they carried off. The master was a man of honor; he gave the whole to the shepherd, saying, "This treasure is yours; it was God who bestowed it on you."

The shepherd took the money, built a house, found a wife, and lived happy and contented. He soon became the richest man, not only in the village, but in the country; for ten leagues around there was not one that could compare with him. He had flocks of sheep, and herds of cattle and horses, with a keeper for each flock and herd, besides much land and money. One Christmas Eve he said to his wife, "Get ready a good stock of wine, brandy, and victuals to carry to the farm to-morrow, that the shepherds may have a feast." This was done, and they all assembled at the farm the next day, when the master said, "My friends, eat, drink, and be merry; I will watch the flocks and herds to-night in your place."

At midnight, as he was keeping guard, the wolves began to howl and the dogs to bark. The wolves said, "Let us come in and harry the cattle, and there will be plenty of fresh meat for you."

And the dogs answered, "Come in; we shall be glad for once to have our fill."

But among the dogs there was an old mastiff with only two fangs in his jaws, who said, "As long as my two fangs are left, you shall not prey on my master's property."

The master heard and understood everything. When morning came, he ordered all the dogs, except the old mastiff, to be taken out and shot. The astonished servants remonstrated, saying it was a great pity to kill so many fine animals, but the master only said, "Do as I bid you."

He set out for home with his wife, the husband mounted

on a handsome gray horse, and the wife on an ambling mare, which was hidden from sight by the long folds of her dress. The husband took the lead, and the wife fell in the rear. The horse turned and said to the mare,

"Hurry! why do you go so slow?"

"Oh, it is easy enough for you to go fast, with only my master to carry, but I have not only my mistress, but all her necklaces, bracelets, skirts, petticoats, satchels and key-bags without end. It needs two yoke of oxen to carry all this paraphernalia."

The husband turned and laughed. His wife, noticing it, pricked on her mare, and, having overtaken her spouse, asked what he was laughing at.

"A mere nothing," said he; "a foolish thought that entered my brain."

This did not satisfy his wife, who insisted on knowing what he laughed at. Tired of her importunity, he cried out at last, "Why can't you leave me in peace? what business is it of yours? I really do not know myself why I laughed."

But the more he stormed, the more she persisted in knowing the cause of his laughter. At last he said, "Know then that if I revealed what I was laughing at, that instant would be my last."

Even this did not stop the dame, who tormented her husband more than ever to tell her. At last they reached home. On alighting from his horse, the husband ordered a bier to be brought. As soon as it was ready, he had it set before the house, and said to his wife,

"Mark me, I shall stretch myself on this bier, and then tell you at what I was laughing, but the instant I have spoken I shall be a dead man."

He stretched himself on the bier, and as he cast a last look around him he saw the old house-dog approaching, with tears in his eyes. The poor man called to his wife to give him a piece of bread. She flung it to the dog, that did not even look at it. The barnyard cock ran up and gulped it down, upon which the dog exclaimed, "Wretched glutton, have you the heart to eat when our master is going to die?"

"Let him die," said the cock, "if he is fool enough to do so. I have a hundred wives; I call them all when I find a kernel of corn, and swallow it as soon as they get there. If any of them should take it into her head to complain I would peck her well for it, while he, who has only one wife, has not wit enough to keep her in order."

No sooner had the husband heard this than he leaped from the bier, seized a stick, and called his wife into the house, saying, "Come, and I will tell you what you want so much to know." He then reasoned with the stick, saying, as each blow fell, "This is it, wife, this is it." Such was the answer he gave her, and never again did the dame ask her husband why he laughed.

POUCINET.

A FINNISH TALE.

I.

ONCE upon a time there was a peasant who had three sons, Peter, Paul, and Jack. Peter was big, fat, red-faced, and dull-witted ; Paul was spare, sallow, envious, and spiteful ; Jack was as sharp as a steel-trap and as fair as a woman, but small—so small that he could have hidden away in his father's great boots, whence he was nicknamed Poucinet.

The peasant's sole worldly wealth was his family, and there was joy in the household when by chance they caught a glimpse there of the shadow of a penny. Black bread was dear, and it was hard to earn a living. As soon as the three children were old enough to begin to work, their father begged them from morning to night to leave the hut where they were born and go out into the world to seek their fortune.

"In other lands," said he, "bread is not always easily earned, but there is some to be had for the getting; while here there is none at all, and the best thing that can happen to you is to die of starvation."

But, lo! a league from the peasant's cabin the king of the country had his palace —a magnificent building, all of wood, with twenty carved balconies and six glass windows. And, behold, suddenly, on a fine summer's night, just over against the windows there sprung from the ground a huge oak, with such thick branches and foliage that it darkened the whole palace. To cut down this giant was no easy task; not an axe could be found that its trunk did not blunt, and for every branch or root that was cut off two sprouted forth in its place. It was in vain that the king offered three bags of dollars to any one who would rid him of this troublesome neighbor. Tired of the struggle, he was

forced to resign himself to the necessity of having the palace lighted at midday.

This was not all. In a country where brooks sprang
from the very stones, there was no water in the royal household. In summer the inmates had to wash their hands in
beer and to shave with honey. This was a shocking state
of affairs, and the prince had promised lands, money, and
the title of marquis to any one who should dig a well in the
courtyard of the castle deep enough to furnish water all the
year round. But no one had been able to win the prize, for
the palace was on high ground, with a solid bed of granite
an inch below the surface.

Now the king had revolved these two ideas in his brain
till he could think of nothing else. Petty prince as he was,
he was just as self-willed as an Emperor of China. It is the
monopoly of royalty. To attain his ends, he distributed
throughout the length and breadth of his kingdom huge
placards, stamped with the royal arms, offering to any one
who should cut down the tree and dig the well nothing less

than the hand of the princess his daughter and half his kingdom. The princess was as beautiful as the day; the half
of a kingdom is never to be despised; and the reward was
enough to tempt the most ambitious. From Sweden and
Norway, from Denmark and Russia, from Great Britain and
the Continent, came a host of sturdy workmen, axe on shoulder and pick in hand. But it was in vain for them to cut
and to chop, to dig and to hew; their labor was all lost.
At every stroke the oak became harder and the granite more
flinty, so that the boldest were forced at last to give up the
task in despair.

II.

One day, when the people in all the country round were
talking of this matter that turned every one's brains, the
three brothers asked themselves why, if their father was
willing, they should not go and try their fortune. It is true
that they hardly hoped to succeed, and aspired neither to
the princess nor half of the kingdom; but who knew whether they might not find a place and a good master at the
court or elsewhere; and this was all they needed. Their
father approved of the plan, and Peter, Paul, and Jack set
out for the king's palace.

On the way, Poucinet skipped along the road, scampering hither and thither like a hound, noticing and studying all he saw, and ferreting into every nook and corner. Insects, weeds, and pebbles, nothing escaped his mouse-like eyes. Every moment he stopped his brothers to ask them the reason for this and that—why the bees burrowed into the flower-cups, why the swallows skimmed the surface of the streams, and why the butterflies flew in zigzag fashion. At all these questions Peter laughed, while Paul shrugged his shoulders, and told him to hold his tongue.

On the way they came to a great forest of firs that covered a mountain, upon the summit of which they heard the sound of an axe and the crash of falling branches.

"I wonder very much why any one is chopping wood on the top of the mountain," said Poucinet.

"I should wonder very much if you did not wonder," answered Paul, harshly. "Everything is wonderful to the ignorant."

"Why, child, any one would think you had never heard of wood-choppers before," said Peter, pinching his little brother's cheek.

"No matter," returned Poucinet, "I am curious to see what is going on up there."

"Go, then," said Paul, "and tire yourself out ; it will be a lesson to you, you conceited imp, who are always wanting to know more than your big brothers."

Poucinet troubled himself little about this remark. He clambered up the mountain, listening for the sound, and making his way in that direction. On reaching the top, what do you think he found there ? An enchanted axe, which, all alone by itself, was cutting down a huge pine-tree.

"Good-morning, Madam Axe," said Poucinet. "Are you not tired of hacking away all alone at that old tree ?"

"For long years I have been waiting for thee, my son,"

answered the axe.

"Well, here I am," replied Poucinet.

And, without being at all astonished, he took the axe, put it in his great leather bag, and skipped merrily down the mountain.

"Did you find anything up there that was so wonderful?" asked Paul, scornfully.

"It was really an axe that we heard," answered the boy.

"I told you so," said Peter; "you have put yourself in a dripping sweat for nothing. You might better have stayed with us."

A little farther on the narrow path wound laboriously among masses of jagged rocks. In the distance, up the cliff, they heard a dull sound, like iron striking the stone.

"I wonder why any one is breaking stone up there," said Poucinet.

"Really," exclaimed Paul, "here is a chicken just out of his shell, who has never heard a woodpecker tapping a hollow tree."

"That's so," said Peter, laughing; "it is nothing but a woodpecker; stay with us, my boy."

"No matter," returned Poucinet; "I am curious to see what is going on up there."

And, behold, he set about clambering up the rocks on his hands and knees, while Peter and Paul laughed at him. On reaching the top of the precipice, what do you think he found there? An enchanted pickaxe, which, all alone, and by itself, was hollowing out the rock as if it had been butter. At every stroke it penetrated more than a foot.

"Good-morning, Madam Pickaxe," cried Poucinet. "Are you not tired of digging away there all alone at that old rock?"

"For long years I have been waiting for thee, my son," answered the pickaxe.

"Well, here I am," rejoined Poucinet."

And, without the least astonishment, he took the pickaxe,

"They stooped to drink from the hollow of their hands."

separated the axe from the handle, put the two pieces in his great leather bag, and skipped merrily down the rocks.

"What miracle did your lordship find up there?" asked Paul, in an insulting tone.

"It was a pickaxe that we heard," answered the boy, and he went on his way without saying anything more.

A little way farther on they came to a brook. The water was cool and clear, and the travellers were thirsty. As they stooped to drink from the hollow of their hands, Poucinet remarked,

"I wonder why there is so much water in such a shallow valley. I should like to know where this brook comes from."

"You conceited fool," cried Paul, "you want to pry into everything. Don't you know that brooks spring from the ground?"

"No matter," said Poucinet; "I am curious to see where this water comes from."

And he followed up the course of the stream in spite of the cries and reproaches of his brothers. He went on and on, while the stream became narrower and narrower. And when he reached the end, what do you think he found? A walnut-shell, from which the water spouted and sparkled in the sun.

"Good-morning, Madam Spring," cried Poucinet. "Are you not tired of staying all alone here in a little corner, spouting water?"

"For long years I have been waiting for thee, my son," answered the walnut-shell.

"Well, here I am!" said Poucinet.

And, without the least astonishment, he took the walnut-shell, stopped it up with moss, so that the water could not flow, put it in his great leather bag, and skipped merrily down the mountain.

"Do you know now where the brook comes from?" cried Peter, as soon as he saw him.

"Yes, brother, from a little hole," answered Poucinet.

"This boy is too bright," said Paul; "he will never live to grow up."

"I have seen what I wished to see," whispered Poucinet to himself, "and I know what I wished to know; I am satisfied." And he rubbed his hands.

III.

At last they reached the king's palace. The oak was larger and more umbrageous than ever; there was no well in the courtyard, and at the palace gate still hung the great placard promising the hand of the princess and one half of the kingdom to any one, noble, burgher, or peasant, that should accomplish the two tasks desired by his majesty. But, as the king was tired of so many useless attempts, which had served no purpose but to drive him to despair, a small placard had been hung under the large one, and on this small placard was written, in red letters,

"Know all men by these presents, that, in his inexhaustible goodness, his majesty the king has deigned to command that any one who does not succeed in cutting down the oak or digging the well shall have his ears cut off on the spot, to teach him to know himself, which is the first lesson of wisdom."

And, in order that every one might profit by this prudent counsel, thirty bloody ears were nailed around this placard, belonging to those who had been lacking in modesty.

On reading the placard, Peter burst out laughing, turned up his mustaches, looked at his arms, with their great muscles, like whip-cords, and swinging his axe twice around his head, with one blow he cut off one of the largest branches of the accursed tree. But, no sooner had it fallen than two thicker and stronger boughs sprouted forth in its place; whereupon the king's guards seized the unlucky wood-chopper, and cut off his ears on the spot.

"You awkward fellow!" exclaimed Paul; and, taking his axe, he walked slowly round the tree, and, seeing a root springing from the ground, he chopped it off at one blow. At the same instant two enormous roots sprang up in its place, from each of which sprouted forth a vigorous branch, full of leaves.

"Seize this wretch!" cried the king, frenzied with rage,

"and, since he did not profit by his brother's example, shave off his ears close to his head."

No sooner said than done. But the double family misfortune did not terrify Poucinet, who resolutely advanced to try his luck.

"Drive away that dwarf!" exclaimed the king; "and if he refuses to go, cut off his ears directly; it will teach him a lesson, and save us from witnessing his folly."

"I beg your pardon, your majesty, a king's word is sacred," said Poucinet. "I have the right to try; it will be time enough to cut off my ears when I fail."

"Go on, then," returned the king, sighing; "but take care that I do not cut off your nose into the bargain."

Poucinet drew the enchanted axe from the bottom of his great leather bag. It was almost as tall as himself, and he had great difficulty in setting it upright, the handle on the ground. "Cut! cut!" he cried.

And, behold, the axe cut, chopped, and split, hewing in all directions, right and left, up and down, trunk, branches, and roots; in a quarter of an hour the tree was in pieces, and there was so much wood that the whole palace was warmed with it for more than a year.

When the tree was hewn down and chopped up, Poucinet approached the king, who was seated with the princess by his side, and bowed gracefully to them both.

"Is your majesty satisfied with your faithful servant?" asked he.

"Yes," said the king, "but I must have my well, or look out for your ears!"

"If your majesty will kindly show me where you wish it placed, I will endeavor once more to please my sovereign," answered Poucinet.

They repaired to the great courtyard of the palace. The king took a raised seat; the princess placed herself a little below her father, and began to look with some anxiety on the diminutive husband sent her by Heaven. She had not dreamed of a spouse of this size. Without troubling himself at all about it, Poucinet took from his great leather bag the enchanted pickaxe, coolly fitted the axe to the handle, and, placing it on the ground at the designated spot, cried,

"Dig! Dig!"

And, behold, the pickaxe splintered the granite, and in less than a quarter of an hour dug a well more than a hundred feet deep.

"Does your majesty think this cistern large enough?" asked Poucinet, with a bow.

"Yes, indeed," said the king; "but there is no water.'

"Let your majesty grant me a minute," returned Poucinet, "and your just impatience shall be satisfied."

Saying this, he took from his great leather bag the walnut-shell, wrapped in moss, and placed it in a large basin, which, in default of water, had been filled with flowers. When the walnut-shell was firmly imbedded in the earth, he cried,

"Spout! spout!"

And, behold, the water spouted forth among the flowers, with a gentle murmur, forming a fountain that filled the whole courtyard with its coolness, and fell again in a cascade in such abundance that in a quarter of an hour the well was full, and it was necessary to hasten to dig a channel to carry off this menacing wealth of water.

"Sire," said Poucinet, bending one knee to the ground before the royal seat, "does your majesty think that I have fulfilled your conditions?"

"Yes, Marquis de Poucinette," replied the king. "I am ready to cede you half my kingdom, or, rather, to pay you the value thereof, by means of a tax which my faithful subjects will be too happy to raise; but to give you the princess and to take you for my son-in-law is another affair, which does not depend on me alone."

"What must I do?" asked Poucinet, haughtily, resting his hand on his hip, and gazing at the princess.

"You shall know to-morrow," said the king. "Meanwhile,

"And behold, the water spouted forth among the flowers with a gentle murmur."

you are our guest, and the best chamber in the palace shall be made ready for you."

The king having gone, Poucinet hastened to find his brothers, who, with their cropped ears, looked like rat-terriers.

"Well, brothers," said he, "was I wrong in keeping my eyes open, and seeking out the reason of things?"

"You have been lucky," answered Paul, coldly. "Fortune is blind and chooses blindly."

"You have done well, my boy," cried Peter. "With or without ears, I rejoice in your good-fortune, and wish our father were here to see it."

Poucinet carried his two brothers away with him, and, being in favor, the chamberlain found a post in the palace the same day for the two cropped varlets.

IV.

On retiring to his apartments, the king could not sleep. A son-in-law like Poucinet was not to his liking. His majesty studied how to avoid keeping his word without seeming to break it. For honest men, this task is difficult. Between his honor and his interest a knave never hesitates, but it is for this very reason that he is a knave.

In his anxiety, the king summoned Peter and Paul. The two brothers alone could tell him the birth, character, and manners of Poucinet. Peter praised his young brother, which delighted his majesty but little ; Paul put him more at his ease by proving to him that Poucinet was nothing but an adventurer, and that it would be absurd for a great prince to feel himself pledged to a low-born wretch.

" The lad is so conceited," said the spiteful Paul, " that he thinks himself able to face a giant. In this district there lives an ogre who is the terror of the neighborhood, and who carries off the sheep and cattle for ten leagues around. Now

Poucinet has said again and again that if he liked he could make this giant his servant."

"We shall see if he will," exclaimed the king; and he dismissed the brothers and slept tranquilly.

The next morning, in the presence of the whole court, the king sent for Poucinet. He came, looking as fair as a lily, as fresh as a rose, and as smiling as the morning.

"My son-in-law," said the king, dwelling upon the words, "a brave man like you cannot marry a princess without giving her a household worthy of her. There is in this forest an ogre who, it is said, is twenty feet high, and who breakfasts every day on an ox. With a laced coat, a cocked hat, gold epaulets, and a halberd fifteen feet long, he would make a porter worthy of a king. My daughter begs you to make her this little present, after which she will see about giving you her hand."

"It is not easy," said Poucinet, "but to please her high-ness I will try."

He went to the kitchen, put in his great leathern bag the enchanted axe, a loaf of bread, a piece of cheese, and a knife, then, throwing it over his shoulder, set out for the forest. Peter wept, but Paul smiled, thinking that, once gone, he would never be heard from again.

On entering the wood, Poucinet looked to the right and the left, but the tall grass prevented him from seeing. Upon this, he began to sing, at the top of his voice, "Ogre! ogre! where are you, ogre? Show your-self! I must have your body or your life! Here I am!"

"And here I am!" cried the giant, with a frightful roar; "wait for me, and I will make but one mouthful of you."

"Don't be in a hurry, my friend," exclaimed Poucinet, in a shrill, pip-ing voice, "I have an hour at your disposal."

The giant turned his head on all sides, astonished to see no one, then, casting down his eyes, he spied a lad, seated on the trunk of a fallen tree, holding a great leather bag between his knees.

"Was it you that broke up my nap, you rascal?" cried the giant, rolling his great flaming eyeballs.

"Yes, my good fellow," said Poucinet; "I have come to take you into my service."

"Ah!" said the giant, who was as dull as he was big, "that is a good joke. I am going to toss you into the crow's nest that I spy up yonder; that will teach you to prowl about my forest."

"Your forest!" returned Poucinet, "it is more mine than yours; if you say another word, I will cut it down in a quarter of an hour."

"Ah!" said the giant, "I should like to see you do that, my little fellow."

Poucinet had placed the axe on the ground. " Cut ! cut !" he cried, and, behold, the axe cut, chopped, split, and hewed to the right and left, and up and down, while the branches rained on the ogre like hail in a storm.

" Enough ! enough !" cried the giant, who began to be alarmed ; " do not destroy my forest. Who are you?"

" I am the famous sorcerer Poucinet, and I have only to speak a word for my axe to chop off your head. You don't know yet whom you have to deal with. Stay where you are."

The giant stood still, greatly puzzled at what he had seen. Poucinet, who was hungry, opened his great leather bag, and took out his bread and cheese.

" What is that white thing?" asked the giant, who had never seen any cheese.

" It is a stone," said Poucinet, beginning to munch it greedily.

" Do you eat stones ?" asked the giant.

" Yes, they are my usual diet ; that is the reason why I do not grow like you, who eat beef ; and that too is why, small as I am, I am ten times stronger than you. Show me the way to your house."

The giant was conquered. He led the way for Poucinet, like a huge dog, and brought him to an immense building.

" Listen !" said Poucinet to the giant ; " one of us must be the master and the other the servant. Let us make a bargain. If I cannot do what you can, I will be your slave ; if you cannot do what I can, you shall be mine."

" Agreed !" said the giant ; " I should like to have a little fellow like you to wait on me. It tires me to think, and you have wit enough for both of us. To begin with, here are my two buckets ; go bring me the water for dinner."

Poucinet raised his head and looked at the buckets.

" ' Enough, enough,' cried the giant, who began to be alarmed, ' do not destroy my forest.' "

They were two immense tuns, each ten feet high and six feet in diameter. It would have been easier to drown in them than to stir them.

"Ah!" said the giant, opening his huge mouth, "you are already nonplussed, my son. Do what I do, and go draw the water."

"What is the use of that?" asked Poucinet; "I will go and fetch the spring, and turn that into the dinner-pot; it will be much easier."

"No, no," cried the giant; "you have already spoiled my

forest; do not meddle with my spring—to-morrow I shall be thirsty. Make the fire and I will bring the water."

Having hung the dinner-pot over the fire, the giant threw in it a whole ox, cut in pieces, with fifty cabbages and a cart-load of carrots. He skimmed it with a frying-pan, and tasted it again and again.

"Come to the table," said he, at length, "and now let me see you do what I do. For my part, I feel hungry enough to eat this whole ox and you into the bargain. You will answer for my dessert."

"Very well," said Poucinet. But before sitting down he slipped under his jacket his great leather bag, so that it fell from his throat to the ground.

The giant ate and ate, and Poucinet was not behind him, only, instead of putting the meat, cabbages, and carrots into his mouth, he slipped them into the bag.

"Oh!" cried the giant, "I can eat no more; I must undo a button of my waistcoat."

"Don't stop yet, you lazy fellow," said Poucinet, shoving half a cabbage under his chin.

"Ah!" cried the giant, "I must undo another button. What an ostrich's stomach you have! Any one could see that you are in the habit of eating stones."

"Go on!" said Poucinet, slipping a huge piece of beef out of sight.

"Ugh!" exclaimed the giant, "I have undone my third button—I feel stuffed. And how is it with you, sorcerer?"

"Bah!" said Poucinet, "nothing is easier than to give one's self a little room."

He took his knife and slit his jacket and bag the whole length of the stomach. "It is your turn," said he to the giant, "do what I do!"

"No, I thank you," answered the giant. "I would rather be your servant; I cannot digest steel."

No sooner said than done. The giant kissed his little master's hand in token of submission; then, lifting him on one shoulder and a large bag of gold on the other, he set out for the palace.

V.

There was a holiday at the palace, and no one was thinking any more of Poucinet than if the giant had eaten him a week before, when suddenly there was heard a terrible uproar, which shook the building to its foundation. It was the giant, who, finding the great gate too small for him, had knocked it down with one blow of his foot. Every one ran to the window, the king with the rest, and saw Poucinet tranquilly seated on the shoulder of his terrible servant, on a level with the second-story balcony, where the court was assembled. He stepped down among them, and, bending his knee before his betrothed, said, " Princess, you wished for a slave; here are two of them."

This gallant speech, which was inserted the next day in the court journal, embarrassed the king not a little at the moment when it was spoken. Not knowing what answer to make, he drew the princess aside in the embrasure of a window and said, " My daughter, I have no excuse for refusing your hand to this daring youth. Sacrifice yourself, for state reasons; princesses do not marry for their inclination alone."

" I beg your pardon," returned she, with a courtesy, "princess or not, every woman wishes to marry to suit her taste. Leave me to defend my rights in my own way.

" Poucinet," she added, aloud, "you are brave and successful, but that is not sufficient to please the ladies."

" I know it," answered Poucinet; " it is necessary besides to do their will and bend to their caprices."

" You are a bright fellow," said the princess. " Since you

are so good at guessing, I propose to you a last ordeal,
which should not terrify you, since you will have me for your
adversary. Let us try which is the cleverer, you or I. My
hand shall be the price of victory."

Poucinet made a low bow. The whole court descended
to the throne-room, where, to the general consternation, they
found the giant seated on the ground. The ceiling being only
fifteen feet high, the poor giant could not stand upright. At
a sign from his young master, he crept to his side, proud
and happy to obey him. It was strength in the service of
intellect.

"We will begin with an extravaganza," said the princess.
"It is said that women do not stick at untruths; let us see
which can tell the greatest falsehood. The one who first
cries, 'That is too much!' will have lost."

"I am at your highness's orders, to lie in jest, or to speak
the truth in earnest," answered Poucinet.

"I am sure," said the princess, "that your farm is not so

large as ours. When two shepherds blow their horns at each
end of the land, neither can hear the other."

"That is nothing," said Poucinet. "My father's estate is
so vast that a heifer that is two months old when she enters
the gate on one side is a full-grown milch cow when she
leaves it on the other."

"That does not astonish me," said the princess. "But you
have not such a huge bull as ours. Two men, seated on its
horns, cannot touch each other with a twenty-foot pole."

"That is nothing," said Poucinet. "The head of my father's bull is so large that a servant perched on one horn
cannot see the man sitting on the other."

"Neither does that surprise me," said the princess. "But
you have not so much milk as we, for we fill daily twenty
tuns each a hundred feet in height, and pile up a mountain of cheeses every week as high as the great pyramid of
Egypt."

"What of that!" said Poucinet. "In my father's dairy
they make such mammoth cheeses that our mare one day having fallen into the mould, we did not find her until after a
week's search. The poor animal had broken her back, and
to use her I was forced to replace her spine by a large fir-
tree, which worked admirably. But one fine morning the fir
put forth a branch in the air, which grew so tall that, on
climbing it, I reached the sky. There I saw a lady dressed in
white, spinning thread from the foam of the sea; I caught
hold of it, when, crack! it snapped, and I fell into a mouse-
hole. There, whom should I find but your father and my
mother, each with a distaff; and your father was so awkward that my mother boxed his ears till his mustaches
shook."

"That is too much!" cried the princess, furious; "my father would never have submitted to such an indignity."

"She said, ' That is too much,' " cried the giant. " Master, the princess is ours."

VI.

"Not yet," said the princess, blushing, " Poucinet, I have three riddles to set you ; guess them, and nothing will be left me to do but to obey my father. Tell me what it is that is always falling and is never broken ?"

"Oh !" said Poucinet, " my mother told me that long ago ; it is a waterfall."

"That is so," said the giant ; " who would have guessed that ?"

"Tell me," said the princess, in a more tremulous voice, " what it is that travels the same road every day, yet never retraces its steps ?"

"Oh !" answered Poucinet, " my mother taught me that long ago ; it is the sun."

"That is right," said the princess, pale with anger. " There remains a last question : what is it that you think and I do not ? what is it that I think and that you do not ? what is it that we both think ? and what is it that neither of us thinks ?"

Poucinet cast down his head and reflected ; he was embarrassed.

"Master," said the giant, "if the question is too hard, don't bother your brains about it. Make a sign, and I will carry off the princess and settle the matter."

"Be silent, slave," answered Poucinet. "Strength can do little, my poor fellow, as you must know. Let me try some other means.

"Madam," said he, after a profound silence, "I scarcely dare guess your riddle, in which, nevertheless, I discern my happiness. I ventured to think that your words would not puzzle me, while you justly thought the contrary. You are good enough to think that I am not unworthy to please you, while I have not the temerity to think so. Lastly, what we both think," added he, smiling, "is that there are greater fools than we in the world; and what neither of us think is that the king, your august father, and this poor giant have as much—"

"Silence!" said the princess. "Here is my hand."

"What is it that you think about me?" asked the king. "I should be glad to know."

"My good father," said the princess, throwing herself on his neck, "we think that you are the wisest of kings and the best of men."

"Right!" returned the king. "I know it. Meanwhile, I must do something for my good people. Poucinet, I make you a duke."

"Long live my master, Duke Poucinet!" cried the giant, in such a voice that it was thought a thunderbolt had fallen upon the palace. Luckily, the only harm done was a general panic and a score of broken window-panes.

VII.

To describe the marriage of the princess and Poucinet would be a useless task. All weddings are alike; the only difference is in the day after. Nevertheless, it would be inexcusable on the part of a faithful historian not to tell how much interest the giant's presence added to the magnificent festival. For example, on coming out of the church, in the excess of his joy the faithful giant could think of nothing better to do than to pick up the bridal carriage and put it on his head, and thus bring back the pair in triumph to the palace. This is one of the incidents that it is well to note, as its like is not seen every day.

In the evening there was a scene of festivity. Feasting, speech-making, epithalamiums, colored glass, fireworks, flowers, and bouquets—nothing was lacking; there was universal rejoicing. In the palace, every one was laughing, singing, eating, drinking, or talking. One man alone, lurking in a corner, solaced himself in a way different from the rest : this was Paul ; he was glad his ears had been cut off, since he was thus made deaf and unable to hear the praises lavished on his brother ; and wished that he were also blind, that he might not see the happiness of the spouses. Unable to bear his thoughts, he at last fled to the woods, where he was devoured by the bears. I wish that all spiteful people might share his fate.

Poucinet was so small that it seemed hard at first for him to command respect ; but his affability and gentleness soon won the love of his wife and the affection of all his people. After the death of his father-in-law he filled the throne for fifty-two years, without any one for a single day desiring a revolution. Incredible as this fact may seem, it is attested by the official chronicle of his reign. He was so shrewd, says the history, that he always divined what would serve and please his subjects, and so good that the pleasure of others was his chief joy. He lived only for the good of those about him.

" The faithful giant could think of nothing better to do than to set the
carriage on his head."

But why praise his goodness? Is it not the virtue of men of wit? Whatever may be said, there is no such thing on earth as stupid people that are good. When one is stupid, he is not good, and when he is good, he is not stupid; trust my long experience. If all the fools in the world are not wicked, which I suspect, all the wicked are fools. This is the moral of my story; if any one finds a better let him go and tell it at Rome.

THE PRUDENT FARMER.

A RAGUSAN TALE.

ONCE upon a time there lived at Ragusa a farmer who
dabbled a little in trade. One day he set out for town to
make a few purchases, taking with him all his money. On
reaching a cross-road he stopped and asked an old man
whom he chanced to find there which route he should take.

"I will tell you for a hundred crowns and no less," answered the stranger; "every piece of advice I give is worth
a hundred crowns."

"Indeed!" thought the farmer, closely observing the foxy-
looking old man. "What kind of advice can it be that is
worth a hundred crowns? It must be something very rare,
for in general you get plenty of advice for nothing; it is true
that it is not worth much more than you give for it. Well!"
said he to the old man, "speak, here is your money."

"Mark me well," resumed the stranger, "the straight road that you see before you is the road of the present; the other one, which makes a curve, is the road of the future. I have some more advice to give you," he added, "but for that you must pay me another hundred crowns."

The farmer reflected long, but finally thought to himself, "Since I have bought the first, I may as well buy the second." And he gave another hundred crowns.

"Listen," said the stranger, "when you are on a journey, and stop at an inn where the host is old and the wine is new, begone quickly, if you would escape harm. Give me another hundred crowns," he added, "I have still something more to tell you."

The farmer reflected, " What can this new piece of advice be ? Bah! since I have bought two, I may as well buy the third one." And he gave his last hundred crowns.

" Heed me well !" said the old man, " if ever you fly in a passion, keep half of your wrath for the morrow, and do not use up all your anger in one day."

The farmer returned home empty-handed.

" What did you buy ?" asked his wife.

" Nothing but three pieces of advice, each of which cost me a hundred crowns," he answered.

"That is just like you, wasting your money, and scattering it to the winds, as usual !"

" My dear wife," said the farmer, gently, " I do not regret my money. Just listen to the sayings which I bought with it."

But his wife shrugged her shoulders at what she styled idle words, and called her husband a fool, who would ruin his household and leave his wife and children to starve.

A short time after, a merchant stopped before the farmer's door, with two wagons full of goods. He had lost his partner on the way, and he offered the farmer fifty crowns if he would take charge of one of the wagons and go with him to town.

"I hope you will not refuse," said the farmer's wife to him, " this time you will earn something, at least."

They set out, the merchant driving the first wagon, and the farmer the second. The weather was bad and the roads heavy, and they travelled with great difficulty. At last they reached the cross-road, where the merchant asked which route they should take.

" That one, which is the road of the future," said the farmer ; "it is longer but it is surer."

The merchant, however, insisted on taking the road of the

present. " I would not go that way for a hundred crowns,"
said the farmer.

They separated, therefore; the farmer, who had taken the
longer road, nevertheless arrived much before his comrade,
with his wagon in good condition. The merchant did not
rejoin him till night; his wagon had fallen in a morass, all
the load had been damaged, and the master had been hurt
into the bargain.

At the first inn they reached the host was old, and a
green branch announced that new wine was sold there cheap.
The merchant wished to stop there for the night.

" I would not do it for a hundred crowns," exclaimed the
farmer, and he departed hurriedly, leaving his companion.
During the evening, a group of young idlers, who had drank
too freely of the new wine, quarrelled for some trifling cause,
knives were drawn, the host, cumbered with years, had not
the strength to separate the combatants, a man was killed,
and, in order to escape the law, the corpse was hid in the
wagon of the merchant. The latter, who had slept well, and

had heard nothing of the affray, rose early to harness his horses. Terrified at finding a dead body in his wagon, he drove off as fast as he could in order to escape a tedious law-suit. But the Austrian police were on his track ; they pursued and overtook him, and while waiting for the case to be brought to trial, threw the merchant in prison and confiscated his goods.

On learning of what had happened to his comrade, the farmer determined at least to save the wagon under his charge, and returned to his own house. On nearing the garden, he saw through the twilight a young soldier seated in his finest plum-tree, coolly munching his favorite fruit. The farmer raised his gun to shoot the thief, when he reflected, " I have paid a hundred crowns to learn that I must not spend all my wrath in one day. Let us wait till to-morrow ; the thief will return."

He made a circuit to enter the house by another way. As he knocked at the door, the young soldier flung himself in his arms, crying, " Father, I have a furlough, and have come to surprise and embrace you."

Said the farmer to his wife, " Now hear what has happened to me, and see whether I paid too dear for my three pieces of advice."

He told them the whole story. As the poor merchant was hung, in spite of all he could do, the farmer found himself the heir of this imprudent man. Enriched thereby, he daily repeated that good advice is never bought too dearly, and for the first time his wife and he are of one and the same mind.

A FEMALE SOLOMON.

A CROATIAN TALE.

There was once upon a time a poor man who lived in a hut alone with his daughter; but this daughter was as wise as Solomon. She went everywhere in search of alms, and also taught her father what to say to obtain what he needed. One day he chanced to solicit aid from the emperor, who, surprised at his manner of speaking, asked him who he was, and who had taught him to express himself in a way so much above his station.

"My daughter, sire," he answered.

"And who taught your daughter?" asked the emperor.

"It was God, as well as our great misery," was the reply.

"Take these thirty eggs to your daughter," said the emperor, "and tell her to hatch chickens from them; if she does not, woe betide her!"

The poor man went to his hut in tears, and told the story to his daughter. She saw at once that the eggs were boiled; but told her father to go to bed, and she would see to everything. He followed her advice; for her part, she took a pot, filled it with water and beans and hung it over the fire; then, next morning, when the beans were boiled, she called her father and told him to take a plough and oxen and plough up the earth by the side of the road where the emperor was to pass.

" And," she added, " when you see the emperor, sow these beans, and say, in a loud voice, ' God bless my boiled beans and make them grow !' Then, if the emperor asks how it is possible for boiled beans to grow, answer that it is as easy as to hatch a chicken from a boiled egg."

The poor man did as he was bid; he ploughed up the ground, sowed the beans, and cried, when he saw the emperor, " God bless my boiled beans and make them grow !" And when the emperor stopped and said, " Poor fool, how is it possible for boiled beans to grow ?" he answered, " Gracious emperor, it is as easy as to hatch a chicken from a boiled egg."

The emperor knew that the daughter had prompted her father to act in this way. He ordered his valets to bring the poor man before him ; then he gave him a small package of hemp, and said, " Take this, and make of it sails, cordage, and all that is needed for a vessel, or else I will cut off your head."

The poor man took the package and returned drowned in tears to his daughter. On hearing what had happened she told him to go to bed, and that she would put matters right. The next day she took a bit of wood, awoke her father, and said,

"Take this match to the emperor, and let him make from it a spindle, a shuttle, and a loom, after which I will do what he asks."

The poor man once more followed his daughter's advice ; he went to the emperor and repeated what he had been bid to say. The emperor was astonished. After a moment's thought he took a goblet, and, giving it to the poor man, said, "Take this goblet to your daughter, and tell her to bale out the ocean, and make of it an arable field."

The poor man obeyed, sighing, and carried the goblet to his daughter, repeating the emperor's message. Again she told him to go to bed, and leave the matter to her. The next day she called him and gave him a bunch of tow, saying,

"Take this to the emperor and let him stop up all the springs and the mouths of all the rivers, after which I will bale out the sea."

When the emperor heard this, he perceived that the maiden was wiser than he. He ordered her to be brought before him, and when they were face to face, asked the question, "My girl, can you tell me what is heard farthest off?"

"Thunder and falsehood are heard farthest off, gracious emperor," she answered.

The emperor thereupon took his beard in his hand and, turning to the courtiers, said, "Guess how much my beard is worth."

When they had all estimated its value, some more and others less, the damsel maintained to their faces that none of them had guessed right, saying, "An emperor's beard is worth three rains in a summer's drought."

The emperor was delighted, and said, "She has guessed nearest of all." He asked her if she would be his wife, adding that he would not let her go until she had consented. The damsel bowed and said,

"Gracious emperor, your will be done! I only ask that you shall give me a writing, in your own hand, declaring that if at any time you grow tired of me and wish to send me away from you and out of the palace, I shall have the right to carry away with me what I love best."

The emperor consented, and gave her a writing sealed with the red wax and great official stamp of the empire.

"An emperor's beard is worth three rains in a summer's drought."

It chanced after a time that the emperor grew tired of his wife, as she had foreseen, and said to her, "I will live with you no longer; leave the palace, and go where you please."

"Illustrious emperor," answered the empress, "I will obey you; only permit me to stay here one night longer, and to-morrow I will go."

The emperor having granted this request, before supper the empress mixed brandy and sweet herbs with the wine, and persuaded him to drink of it, saying,

"Drink and be merry; to-morrow we part; and, believe me, I shall be happier than on my wedding-day."

The emperor had scarcely swallowed the beverage when he fell fast asleep. The empress had him taken at once to a carriage which she had ready, and carried him away with her to a grotto hewn in the rock. On awaking, he rubbed his eyes, and looking around him at the strange spectacle, cried, "Where am I, and who brought me here?"

"It was I," answered the empress.

"Why did you do this? Did I not tell you that you were no longer my wife?"

"It is true that you said so," returned she, extending to him a paper, "but do you remember what you promised me in this writing? On quitting the palace I had a right to take away with me what I loved best in it, and this dearest thing is you."

At these words the emperor's heart melted; he embraced her, and they returned to the palace together, never more to part.

13

DAME GUDBRAND.

A NORWEGIAN TALE.

THERE was once an old man called Gudbrand of the Hill, who lived in a lonely cottage on a distant hillside.

Now it must be known that this Gudbrand had an excellent wife, which sometimes happens. But what happens far more seldom was that Gudbrand understood the value of such a treasure. The husband and wife lived peacefully together, enjoying their common happiness, and troubling themselves neither about the lack of money nor their advancing years. Everything that Gudbrand did, his wife declared to be just what she most wanted; so that the good man could not move or change a single thing in the house without his wife's thanking him for having foreseen and accomplished her wishes.

They led an easy life, moreover; the farm belonged to them, and they had a hundred dollars in their drawer, and two good milch cows in their stable. They lacked for nothing, and could grow old without fearing want and wretchedness, or needing the pity or assistance of their neighbors. One evening, as they were talking together by the fireside of their work and their plans, Dame Gudbrand said to her husband,

"My dear, a happy thought strikes me. Why not take one of our cows to town and sell it? The other one will

" He lived in a lonely cottage on a distant hillside."

give us all the milk and butter we need, and what is the use of wearing ourselves out for others? We have no children, and money lying idle ; and it is better to save our strength. You will always find enough to do to keep you busy at home, mending tools and furniture, and I shall have more time to sit by you with my spindle and distaff."

Gudbrand, as usual, thought his wife was quite right, and set off early the next morning for town, with his cow. But it was not market-day, and he found no one ready to buy her.

"Well, well," said he to himself, "I have only to drive her home again ; I have plenty of straw and fodder for her, and the road is no longer going than coming ;" and with these words, he tranquilly turned his face homeward.

After a few hours' walk, just as he was beginning to feel a little tired, he met a man riding a horse to town—a superb-looking animal, all saddled and bridled.

"The way is long, and darkness is coming on fast," thought Gudbrand ; "I shall not get home to-night with my cow, and my wife will be worried. How proud she would be to see me come prancing into the yard on this horse, like a bailiff!" And with this thought, he stopped the rider, and exchanged his cow for the horse.

Once in the saddle he had some misgivings. Gudbrand

was old and heavy, and the horse was young, fiery, and skittish. In half an hour Gudbrand was on foot, with the bridle on his arm, trying hard to hold the frisky animal, that tossed his head in the wind, and reared and pranced at every stone by the wayside. "It is a bad bargain," thought Gudbrand; when, just at that instant, he spied a countryman leading a pig as fat as butter, whose belly touched the ground.

"I have often heard my wife say, "thought Gudbrand, "that a humble nail that is of use is worth more than a sparkling diamond that is good for nothing." And he exchanged his horse for the pig.

It was a happy thought, but the good man had counted without

his host. Master Porker was tired, and would not budge an-other step. Gudbrand talked, coaxed, and swore, but all in vain. He dragged the pig by the snout, he pushed him from behind, he beat him on all sides, and had his trouble for his pains. The creature lay in the dust like a ship stuck in the mud. The farmer was in despair, when a man passed leading a goat, which, with its

udders full of milk, pranced, ran, and curveted with an agility charming to behold.

"Just what I want," cried Gud-

brand; "I had rather have that lively, merry goat, than this stupid, vile
beast." And thereupon, without giving the matter a second thought, he
exchanged the pig for the goat.

Everything went smoothly for the
space of half an hour. The long-
horned damsel led on Gudbrand, who
at first laughed at her pranks. But
when one is past twenty, he soon tires
of climbing rocks; and the farmer, chancing to meet a shepherd watching his flock, was easily persuaded to exchange
his goat for a sheep. "I shall have just as much milk,"
thought he, "and this animal at least will be quiet, and will
not tire my wife
and me."

Gudbrand had
judged rightly;
there is nothing
more placid than
a sheep. She
played no pranks,
and did not try to butt him; but she would not go on, and
stood bleating for her sisters. The more Gudbrand pulled,
the more she endeavored to return to the flock, and the
more pitifully she moaned.

"The whimpering fool!" cried Gudbrand. "She is as headstrong and as whining as my neighbor's wife. Who will take this bleating, crying, groaning beast off my hands? I would sell her at any price."

"It is a bargain," said a peasant who was passing. "Take this fine, fat goose, which is far better than a sheep that will moan itself to death in an hour."

"Agreed," said Gudbrand ; "a live goose is worth more than a dead sheep." And he carried off the goose with him.

This, however, was no easy task. The bird was an uneasy companion. Frightened at being off the ground, it fought lustily with wings, claws, and beak, till Gudbrand was tired of the struggle.

"Pooh !" said he, "a goose is a hateful bird ; my wife never would have one in the house."

And, thereupon, at the first farmhouse where he stopped, he exchanged the goose for a handsome cock, with

gay plumage, and fine spurs and
comb. This time he was satisfied
with his bargain. The cock, it is
true, screamed from time to time,
in a voice too shrill to please sen-
sitive ears, but as his legs were
tied together and he was carried
head downward, he soon submitted to his fate. The only trouble

was that it was growing late. Gudbrand, who had set out
before daybreak, found himself at evening hungry and pen-
niless. He had still a long way to go ; his legs were falter-
ing, and his stomach was crying for food. He was equal to
the occasion. At the first inn, he sold his cock for half a
dollar, and as he had a good appetite, spent it to the last
penny in satisfying his hunger.

"After all," thought he, "of what use would a cock be to
me after I had perished of starva-
tion ?"

On nearing home, Gudbrand began to reflect on the strange way
in which his journey had turned
out. Before entering his house, he
stopped at his neighbor's, Grizzled
Peter.

"Well, Gudbrand," said Peter,
"what luck did you have in town ?"

"So, so," said he ; "I cannot say that I have been very
lucky, but neither have I reason to complain." And he
told him all that had happened.

"Well, neighbor," exclaimed Peter, "you have made a fine
mess of it ! What will your wife say to you ? May God protect you ! I would not be in your shoes for ten dollars."

"Why," said Gudbrand, "matters might have turned out much worse with me; as it is, I am well, and at peace in body and soul. And whether I have been wise or foolish, I have such a good wife that she will be perfectly satisfied with everything I have done."

"I hear what you say, neighbor, and marvel at it, but with all due respect to you, I don't believe a word of it."

"Will you bet that I am wrong?" said Gudbrand. "I have a hundred dollars in my drawer at home; I will venture twenty-five of them; will you do the same?"

"Yes, indeed," said Peter.

The bargain concluded, the two friends entered Gudbrand's house. Peter stood at the chamber-door to listen.

"How are you, dame?" said Gudbrand.

"Thank God, you are home again!" exclaimed his wife; "I was beginning to be so uneasy about you. How are you, and what success have you had in town?"

"So, so," said Gudbrand; "I could find no one to whom to sell our cow, so I exchanged her for a horse."

"For a horse!" exclaimed his wife; "what an excellent idea. I thank you with all my heart. Now we can go in

" 'Good-evening, dame,' said Gudbrand."

our wagon to church, like so many people who look down upon us, and are no better than we. If we choose to keep a horse and feed it, it is nobody's business ; we have a perfect right to do so. Where is the horse ? He must be put into the stable."

"I did not bring him home," said Gudbrand ; "on the way I changed my mind and traded him for a pig."

"Why," said his wife, "that is just what I should have done in your place. A thousand thanks, my dear. Now, when the neighbors drop in, I shall have a bit of bacon to offer them, like other people. What do we want of a horse? The neighbors would say, 'See those proud folks, looking down on us who have to walk to church.' Come, we must put the pig in his sty."

"I did not bring the pig, either," said Gudbrand ; "on the way I changed him for a goat."

"Bravo !" cried his wife, "what a wise and prudent man you are ! Now I think of it, what should we have done with a pig? Folks would have pointed their fingers at us, saying, 'Look at those people, who eat up all they make !' But with my goat I shall have milk and cheese, to say nothing of kids. Make haste and put the goat in the stable."

"But I did not bring the goat, ' said Gudbrand ; "on the way I exchanged it for a sheep."

"That is just like you !" cried his wife ; "you did this for my sake. I am too old to climb over hills and rocks after a goat. But with a sheep I shall have milk and wool besides. Put the sheep in the stable."

"I did not bring the sheep, either," said Gudbrand ; "on the way I changed it for a goose."

"Thank you with all my heart," said the good woman "what should I have done with a sheep? I have neither spinning-wheel nor loom ; weaving is hard work, and when

the cloth is woven, it must be cut out and made. It is
much easier to buy ready-
made clothing, as we have
always done. But a goose
—a fat goose—is just what I
wanted; I need down for our
bed ; and I have always had
a longing for once in my life
to eat a roast goose. Come,
let us put the goose in the
barn-yard."

"But neither did I bring
the goose home," said Gudbrand; "on the way I changed
it for a cock."

"My dear," said his wife,
"you are wiser than I. A
cock is really useful ; it is
better than a clock, which
must be wound every week.
A cock crows every morning
at four o'clock, and tells us
that it is time to praise God
and go to work. After all,
of what good would a goose
have been to us? I do not
know how to cook it ; and as
for our bed, thank God, there
is plenty of moss as soft as
down. Put the cock in the
barn-yard."

"I did not bring the cock,
either," said Gudbrand, "for at nightfall I found myself as

hungry as a hunter, and had to sell the cock for half a dollar, without which I should have died of starvation."

"God be praised for giving you this happy thought!" cried his wife. "My dear, you have done everything just as I wished. What do we need of a cock? We are our own masters; no one has a right to order us about, and we can lie in bed as late as we like. Now that you are here, my dear husband, I am happy. I need but one thing, and that is, to know that you are by my side."

Upon this Gudbrand opened the door, and called, "Neighbor Peter, what did I tell you? Go, fetch your twenty-five dollars." And he kissed his old wife on both cheeks with as much pleasure and more tenderness than if she had been twenty years old.

GRIZZLED PETER.

A NORWEGIAN TALE.

THE story does not end here. Every medal has its ob-
verse side. The day would not appear so bright if it were
not blotted out by the night. However good and perfect all
women may be, there are, nevertheless, a few who are not
always as easy-tempered as Dame Gudbrand. Need I say
that this is the husband's fault? If he always gave way,
would he ever be contradicted? "Give way!" I hear some
whiskered gentleman exclaim. Yes, of course; else hear
with what you are threatened. A Norwegian experience
may be useful elsewhere.

Grizzled Peter bore no resemblance to his neighbor, Good-
man Gudbrand. He was petulant, imperious, choleric, and
about as impatient as a dog from whom a bone is snatched,
or a cat that is seized by the nape of the neck. He would
have been unbearable if Heaven, in its mercy, had not given
him a wife worthy of him. This good woman was headstrong, quarrelsome, rasping, shrewish, and always ready to

be silent when her husband wanted to talk, or to rail when he wished to be at peace. It was great good luck for Grizzled Peter to have such a treasure. Without his wife, how could he have ever known that patience is not the merit of fools, and that gentleness is the chief of virtues.

One night, in harvest, when he returned home after fifteen hours' hard labor, more ill-tempered than ever, loudly asking if supper was not ready, and furiously scolding at women and their laziness,

"Hold your tongue, Peter," said his wife. "Would you like to change places? To-morrow I will go harvesting and you shall keep house. We will see which has the harder work, and does it better."

"Done!" answered Peter. "You will learn, for once, by experience, what your poor husband suffers. It may teach you to respect him ; you need the lesson."

The next morning, at daybreak, his wife set out, her rake over her shoulder and her sickle by her side, rejoiced to see the sun rise, and singing like the lark.

Grizzled Peter was a little surprised to find himself alone in the house. He made the best of it, however, and set to work to churn the butter, as if he had been accustomed to it all his life. One soon gets heated at a new trade. Peter's throat was dry, and he went down cellar to draw some beer. He had just taken the spigot out of the cask, and was about to put in the spout, when he heard overhead the grunting of the pig, who was ravaging the kitchen.

"My butter is lost!" cried Peter. He rushed up the cellar steps, four at a time, with the spigot in his hand. Such a spectacle as met his sight! The churn was overturned, the cream was on the ground, and the pig was wallowing in floods of milk. A wiser man would have lost patience. Peter flung himself upon the animal, that ran away grunting. The thief paid dearly for his crime, for his master seized him on the way, and dealt him such a blow on the head  with the spigot that he fell stark dead on the spot.

As he gazed at his bloody work, Peter bethought himself  that he had not closed the bunghole, and that the beer was still running. He rushed down cellar. Fortunately, the beer was running no longer; it is true that not a drop was left in the cask.

It was necessary to begin anew and churn the butter if he wished to have any dinner. Peter went to the dairy, and found cream enough there, fortunately, to repair the accident of the morning.

He set about churning with all his might, when he suddenly remembered, rather late in the day, that the cow was still

in the stable, and had had nothing yet to eat or drink, though the
sun was now high in the heavens.
He started for the stable, but experience had made him wise.

"There is the baby crawling
on the floor," he thought; "he
will be sure to upset the churn if
I leave it here."

He took the churn on his back,
and went to draw water for the
cow. The well was deep, and
the bucket did not fill. Peter became impatient, and leaned
over to pull the rope, when, pop! a deluge of cream from
the churn poured over his head and
into the well.

"Oh, dear!" cried Peter; "I
shall have no butter to-day. I must
think now of the cow. It is too
late to drive her to pasture, but
there is a fine growth of hay that
has not been cut on the thatched
roof. She will lose nothing by staying at home."

Having taken the cow from the
stable, it was not difficult to get
her on the roof. The house being
built in a hollow, the thatch on one
side was nearly on a level with the
ground, and, with the help of a
broad plank, the cow was easily installed in her aerial pasture.

"He let the rope carefully down the kitchen chimney."

Peter could not stay on the roof to watch the cow. He had to make soup and carry it to the reapers. But being a

prudent man, and not wishing to expose his cow to the danger of breaking her bones, he tied a long rope around her neck, which he carefully lowered down the kitchen chimney; this done, he returned to the kitchen, and fastened the rope around his leg. "Now," thought he, "I can be quite sure that the animal will be quiet, and that nothing will happen to her."

He filled the pot, put into it a good piece of bacon, some vegetables, and water, hung it over the fagots, lighted a match, and blew the fire, when, presto! the cow slipped from the roof and dragged our gentleman up the chimney, head downward and heels in air. There is no knowing what would have happened to him had not a strong iron bar luckily stopped him on the way. There they both hung between heaven and earth, Peter and the cow, he in the chimney and she from the roof, both

shrieking and groaning frightfully.

Happily, the good wife had no more patience than her husband. After waiting three sec-
onds for the soup to be brought
her at the usual time, she ran
home as if the house were on
fire. At the sight of the cow
suspended from the roof she
drew her sickle and cut the
rope. It was a great joy for
the poor animal to find herself
once more upon the ground she
loved ; and it was no less fortunate for Peter, who was not
in the habit of viewing the
heavens feet in air, and who
fell head foremost into the pot.
But luck seemed to be on his
side that day : the fire had not
caught, the water was cold, and
the pot hung awry, so that he
escaped with honor from this
trying ordeal with no other accident than a scratched forehead, grazed nose, and two cut
cheeks. Happily, nothing was
broken but the dinner-pot.

On entering the kitchen and
seeing her husband standing
abashed and bloody, in the
prevailing disorder, the dame
stuck her arms akimbo, and
exclaimed,

"Well, which of us is it that is always right? I have

"The dame stuck her arms akimbo, and exclaimed, 'Well, which of us
is it that is always right?'"

done my work in the harvest-field, and here I am! And
you, Mr. Cook, Mr. Shepherd, Mr. Housekeeper, where is the
butter, where is the beer,
where is the pig, where
is the cow, where is our
dinner? If the baby is
not dead, it is not your
fault! Poor little one,
if you had not your
mother!" Clasping the
baby in her arms, tears
came to her relief. Is
not sensibility the tri-
umph of woman, and
are not tears the triumph of sensibility?

Peter bore the storm sulkily, but in silence. He did well;
resignation befits great minds. But a few days after the
neighbors perceived that he had changed the motto of his
house. Instead of two clasped hands bearing a heart encir-
cled with a blue ribbon and surmounted by an eternal flame,
he had painted on the front of the cottage a hive surrounded
with bees, with the following inscription:

> " Bees sting sharp,
> But evil tongues sharper."

It was his only vengeance for this day of defeat.

THE TAILOR'S DAUGHTER.

A SENEGAL TALE.

THERE was, once upon a time, a Senegal tailor, who had a daughter as dazzling as the sun. All the youths in the neighborhood were in love with her beauty, and two of them went to her and asked for her hand. The girl, like a well-trained daughter, made them no answer, but called her father, who listened to them, and said:

"It is late; go home, and come again to-morrow. I will tell you then which of you shall have my daughter."

At daybreak the next morning the young men were at his door.

"Here we are," they cried; "remember what you promised us yesterday."

"Wait," said the tailor; "I must go out and buy a piece of cloth; when I return, you will hear what I expect you to do."

He soon returned, and, calling his daughter, said to the young men,

"My sons, there are two of you, and I have but one daughter. I cannot give her to both of you, and must refuse one. You see this piece of cloth; I will cut from it two pairs of breeches, exactly alike; each of you shall make one of them, and the one that finishes first shall be my son-in-law."

Each of the rivals took his task, and prepared to set to work under the tailor's eyes. The latter said to his daughter, "Here is thread; you can thread the needles for the workmen."

The girl obeyed; she took the spool and sat down by the youths. But the pretty witch was full of cunning; her father did not know which one she loved, neither did the young men, but, for her part, she knew very well. The tailor went out, the girl threaded the needles, and her suitors set to work. But to the one she loved she gave short needleful, while she gave long needleful to his rival. Both sewed zealously; at eleven o'clock the work was scarcely half done, but at three in the afternoon the young man with the short needleful had finished his task, while the other was far behind. When the tailor returned, the victor carried him the finished breeches. His rival was still sewing.

"My children," said the father, "I did not wish to show any partiality between you, for which reason I divided the cloth into two equal parts, and gave each a fair chance. Are you satisfied?"

"Perfectly," answered they. "We understood your meaning, and accepted the trial; what is to be will be!"

But the tailor had reasoned to himself: "He who finishes his task first will be the better workman, and consequently the one better fitted to support his household." It did not occur to him that his daughter might outwit him by giving the longer needleful to the one she did not wish to win. Woman's wit decided the contest, and the girl chose her husband herself.

14

DAME WEASEL AND HER HUSBAND.

A NUBIAN TALE.

DAME WEASEL brought a son into the world. She called
her husband and said, "Go get me the kind of swaddling-
clothes I want, and bring them here to me."

The husband listened to his wife with a puzzled air, and
asked, "But what kind of swaddling-clothes do you want?"

"I want the skin of an elephant," snapped the weasel.

The poor husband stood agape in amazement, wondering
if his wife had not lost her wits, till the angry weasel flung
the baby in his arms, and rushed out, with a toss of her
head.

She went straight to the Earth-worm and said, "Neighbor,
I have a field covered with turf; come and help me dig it up."

The Worm once busy at work, Dame Weasel went to the
Hen, and said, "Cousin, my field is full of worms, we need
your help in getting rid of them."

The Hen ran thither without waiting for another word,
hastily gobbled up the Worm, and began scratching in the
dirt for more.

A little farther on the Weasel met the Cat; "My friend,"
said she, "there are some hens in my field, and it might be
to your advantage to take a turn that way while I am gone."

A moment after, the Cat had devoured the Hen.

While the Cat was thus regaling himself, the Weasel said
to the Dog, "Master, will you allow the Cat to lord it over

that field?" The furious Dog rushed on the Cat and strangled him, determined that there should be no other ruler there than himself.

The Lion, passing that way, Dame Weasel bowed to him respectfully. "My lord," said she, "do not go near that field, it belongs to the Dog;" upon which the Lion, blinded with jealousy, flung himself on the Dog and tore him to pieces.

The Elephant came next. Dame Weasel entreated his help against the Lion, and begged him to come into her territory as a protector. But he little knew the treachery of the Weasel, who had digged a deep pit there and covered it with boughs. The Elephant fell into the snare, and was killed by the fall, while the Lion, who was afraid of the Elephant, fled to the forest.

The Weasel then stripped off the Elephant's skin, and showed it to her husband, saying, "I asked you in vain for this skin; with God's help I have obtained it myself, and I bring it to you."

The husband of Dame Weasel had not suspected before that his wife was more cunning than all the beasts of the earth, still less, that she was more cunning than he. He was convinced of it at last; and hence came the saying, "He is as cunning as a weasel."

THE SUN'S DAUGHTER.

A GREEK FAIRY TALE.

THERE was once a woman who could not be comforted because she had no children. One day she said to the Sun,

"Good Sun, if you will but give me a daughter, you may take her back when she is twelve years old."

The Sun immediately sent a daughter to the good woman.

She named her Letiko, and cherished her for twelve years like the apple of her eye. But one day, when Letiko was gathering herbs, the Sun came to her and said, "My child, when you go home, tell your mother to remember what she promised me."

Letiko went home and said to the good woman, " Mother, as I was gathering herbs, a handsome young prince came and bade me tell you to remember what you had promised him."

At this message, the good woman trembled and turned pale ; then set instantly to work to shut the doors and windows, and stop up the holes and crevices, that the Sun might not make his way into the house and carry off Letiko.   Unhappily she forgot the keyhole, and the Sun sent one of his beams through it, which seized Letiko, and bore her away.

The Sun was not a bad master, but Letiko could not forget, in his service, the mother she had lost.

One day the Sun sent her to the barn for some hay.   Letiko

seated herself on the sheaves, and sighed, " As this hay is crushed beneath my feet, so my heart is crushed by the loss of my mother." She stayed so long in the barn that the Sun called to her, " Letiko, what are you doing there?"

" My shoes are so large that I cannot walk," she answered. Upon which the Sun made her smaller shoes.

Another day the Sun sent her for water. On reaching the spring, Letiko sighed, " As this water moans as it falls, so moans my heart for my poor mother."

She stayed so long at the spring that the Sun called to her, " Letiko, what are you doing there?" She said, " My skirt is so long that I cannot walk." Upon which the Sun cut off the hem of her skirt.

Another time the Sun sent her for a pair of sandals. On her way back she sat down by the roadside, and sighed, " As this leather creaks in my hand, so does my heart cry out for my poor mother."

She remained seated there so long that the Sun called to her, " Letiko, what are you doing there?"

" My hat is so large that it falls over my eyes, and hinders me from walking."

Upon which the Sun cut off the brim of her hat.

At last the Sun saw that Letiko was sorrowful. He sent her once more to the barn for hay ; but listened at the door and heard the child cry for her mother. He then called to him two foxes, and said,

" Will you take Letiko back home?"

" With pleasure."

" But if you are hungry and thirsty, what will you eat and drink on the way."

" We will eat the child's flesh and drink her blood," answered the honest foxes.

When the Sun heard this, he said to himself, "Good people, you will not do for me." He thanked the foxes, and called two hares.

" Will you take Letiko back to her mother?"

" With pleasure."

" But if you are hungry and thirsty, what will you eat and drink on the way?"

"We will eat the grass of the fields and drink the water of the springs."

"Good, take the child; I trust her to you."

And, behold, the hares set out with Letiko; but the way was long, and they were hungry.

"Dear Letiko," said the hares to the young girl, "climb this tree, and stay there till we have satisfied our appetite."

Letiko climbed the tree, and the hares ran to the forest.

They were hardly out of sight, when a lamia appeared beneath the tree—this is what an ogress is called in Greece. She was a horrible old witch, with only one eye, in the middle of her forehead, and a huge mouth with two great tusks. "Letiko! Letiko! come down and see what pretty shoes I have on!" she cried.

"Mine are as pretty as yours."

"Come down, I am in haste, my house is not swept."

"Go and sweep it, and come back when it is done."

The lamia ran home and hurried back as fast as she could. "Letiko! Letiko!" she cried, "come down and see what a handsome sash I have on."

"My sash is handsomer than yours."

"If you do not come quickly, I will break down the tree and eat you up."

"Break it down first and eat me up afterwards."

And, behold! the ogress shook the tree, without being able to stir it. "Letiko! Letiko! make haste, I must go and feed my babies."

"Go and feed them, and come back when you have done."

The monster gone, Letiko cried, "Help! my hares, help!" And one of the hares said to the other, "Brother, do you hear? The child is calling us." They came running like the wind. Letiko sprang down from the tree, and all three took to their heels.

The witch hurried back as fast as she could, but the bird had flown, whether east, west, north, or south, she knew not.

She saw some men working in the fields, and went to them, but they were as deaf as posts.

"Have you seen any one go by?" asked she.

"We are planting beans," they answered.

"I asked you if you had seen any one go by?" she cried, in a furious tone.

"Letiko rushed in first, followed by the hares."

"What is the matter?" replied the good men; "are you deaf? we are planting beans, do you hear? beans, beans, beans!"

When Letiko approached the house, the dog scented her, and cried, "*Bow, wow, wow!* here is Letiko!" The cat, that was roaming on the roof, spied the child from afar, and began to call, "*Miaow, miaow!* here is Letiko!" The poor mother answered, "Hush, cruel beasts, would you kill me with grief?"

The cock, stretching up his neck and head, saw the child in turn, and crew, "*Cock-a-doodle-doo! Cock-a-doodle-doo!* here is Letiko." And the poor mother sobbed, "Hush, cruel bird, would you kill me with grief?"

The three friends reached the door, but the ogress was at their heels, and had them just within her grasp. Letiko rushed in first, followed by the hares, one after the other, but the last one left the hair of his tail in the witch's clutches. On seeing this, the poor mother clasped Letiko to her breast, and cried, "Welcome! my good hares, you have brought my daughter back in safety, and in return I will dye your tails silver." And ever since that day all the hares have had silver tails.

THE LITTLE MAN.

THERE was once a little gentleman who every day grew twenty-four hours older. But when he went to the inn to drink a glass of wine or a schooner of beer, the inn-keeper always greeted him with, "Good-morning, my little man!" which vexed him greatly.

One morning he went to the shoemaker, to have a pair of high heels put on his boots. No sooner had he entered the shop than the shoemaker exclaimed, "Good-morning, my little man; what can I do for you to-day?"

"Master Crispin," he answered, "hasten to put a pair of

heels on my boots, and let them be high enough to make people stop calling me little man. I am tired of it."

The shoemaker set to work, and when he had finished and been paid, "Good-bye, my little man," said he, "if you are satisfied, remember me another time."

The little gentleman was greatly vexed that the shoe-maker had no more respect for his own work. "It will be different with the inn-keeper," he thought ; "he will open his eyes, and greet me by another name."

He entered the inn, stamping his feet, and standing as straight as if he had swallowed a bayonet. As soon as the inn-keeper saw him, he cried, "Good-morning, my little man ; what will you have, beer or wine ?"

Fancy the vexation of the little gentleman that his heels had produced no more effect! He hastened to the hatter, to buy the tallest hat that could be found. He had not let go the door-knob before the hatter greeted him with,

"Good-morning, my little man, what can I do for you to-day?"

"I want a hat tall enough to make people stop calling me little man; it vexes me beyond measure."

The hatter gave him a hat that might have served for a grenadier, took his money, and thanked his customer. "Good-bye, my little man, remember me next time."

The little man was angry that the hatter paid so little respect to his own wares. "Bah!" thought he, "it will be different at the inn." He hastened thither and entered the bar-room, his hat on his head like an Englishman.

"Good-morning, my little man," said the inn-keeper, "what will you have, beer or wine?"

It is needless to say how much the little man was vexed. What was the use of having such high heels under his feet, and such a tall hat on his head! And how was it that, in spite of all these dearly bought advantages, every one persisted in calling him little man?

Right and left, up and down, he asked all he met why he was still called little man, in spite of his heels and hat, but no one could or would tell him. This vexed him horribly.

"How stupid I am!" thought he; "if the people here know nothing, I will go to Rome and ask the pope, who knows everything."

No sooner said than done ; he packed his valise, and set out for Rome.

On the way he stopped at a tavern to pass the night. " Good-day, my little man," said the host ; "where are you going at this pace ?"

" I am going to Rome to see the pope," answered the little gentleman, ill-humoredly. " The pope will tell me why, in spite of my high heels and tall hat, every one takes the liberty of calling me little man. It makes me furious."

" Bravo !" cried the host. " I will go along with you. I, too, have something to ask the pope. I should like to know why every one calls me the poor tavern-keeper. John, you lazybones, pack my valise, I am going to Rome."

" Master, I am going too," said the hostler. " I should like to ask the pope why every one, without knowing me, calls me lazybones."

On reaching Rome, the three friends asked an audience of the pope. They were received in a 'drawing-room, in which there was a large mirror.

The pope listened to them kindly, and said to the tavern-keeper,

" Turn your back to this mirror ; then look over your left shoulder, and tell me what you see in the glass."

" I see," cried the tavern-keeper, " ten or twelve women, sitting round a table, drinking coffee and chattering. Why ! there is my wife. I'll warrant she will not lose a word of the gossip."

" Well, my son," said the pope, " as long as your wife spends her time in this way, away from home, you will be called a poor tavern-keeper, and you will stay a poor tavern-keeper."

It was the hostler's turn. He placed himself in the same position, and looked over his left shoulder.

" Holy Father !" he cried, " I see dogs chasing a hare.

They think to catch him ; ho ! ho ! Dash and Rover, you
did not get up early enough, the hare is too fast for you !"

"Well, my son," said the pope, "when you run as fast as
this hare the first time an order is given you, be sure that
no one will call you lazybones any longer."

After the hostler came the little gentleman. He too
turned his back to the glass, and looked over his left shoulder. The pope asked him what he saw.

"I see nothing but myself," answered the little man.

"Do you see yourself larger than you are?"

"No," said the little man, "I see myself just as I am, neither smaller nor larger."

"In that case, my son," rejoined the pope, "I have but one piece of advice to give you : to have yourself measured until you have grown. When you are tall, you will no longer be called little man."

The little gentleman retired discontented, it is said, in which he was wrong. But how many there are who are no wiser than he! How many there are who wish to soar above their shadow, who think to add to their stature by borrowed plumes, and who need to go to Rome to see themselves just as they are between their hats and their heels!

FALSEHOOD AND TRUTH.

AN OLD SPANISH FABLE.

In olden times, Falsehood and Truth agreed to live together like a pair of friends. Truth was a good soul, simple, timid, and confiding; Falsehood was plausible, brilliant, and dashing. One commanded, and the other always
obeyed. As may be supposed, everything went on smoothly
in such a delightful partnership.

One day Falsehood suggested to Truth that it would be
well to plant a tree that would give them blossoms in spring,

shade in summer, and fruit in autumn. Truth was pleased with the plan, and the tree was set out directly.

No sooner had it begun to grow than Falsehood said to Truth : " Sister, let us each choose a share of the tree. Possessions held too closely in common breed strife ; short accounts make long friends. There are the roots, for example ; it is they that support and nourish it ; they are shel-

tered from wind and weather ; why do you not take them ? To oblige you, I will content myself, for my part, with the branches, that grow in the open air, at the mercy of birds, beasts, and men, wind, heat, and frost. There is nothing that we would not do for those we love."

Truth, abashed by such goodness, thanked her comrade, and burrowed under ground, to the great joy of Falsehood, who found himself alone among mankind, and able to reign at his ease.

The tree shot up fast; its great boughs spread shade and coolness far and wide, and it soon put forth blossoms fairer than the rose. Men and women hastened from all sides to admire the marvel. Perched upon the topmost branch Falsehood harangued them, and soon charmed them with his honeyed words. He taught them that society is nothing but falsehood, and that men would be ready to tear each other to pieces if they always spoke the truth. "There are three ways to succeed here below," added he: " by simple falsehood, as when the vassal says to his lord, ' I respect and love you ;' by double falsehood, as when he exclaims, ' May the thunderbolts of Heaven fall on me if I am not your most faithful servant ;' and by triple falsehood, as when he repeats, ' My goods, my arm, and my life all are my lord's ;' and then deserts his master at the moment of danger." The good apostle gave these lessons in so airy a manner, and illustrated them by such fine examples, that all who heard him were intoxicated with his words ; they jeered at those who did not applaud, and even began to doubt themselves. For a hundred leagues around, nothing was talked of but Falsehood and his wisdom ; it was proposed to make him king. As to good Truth, who lay crouching in her den, no one gave her a thought ; she might die forgotten.

Abandoned as she was by all, she was forced to live on whatever she could find under ground ; and while Falsehood was enthroned among verdure and flowers, the poor mole gnawed the bitter roots of the tree she had planted. She gnawed them so deep that one day, when Falsehood, more eloquent than usual, was addressing an innumerable multitude, the wind rose slightly, and suddenly blew down the tree, that had no longer any roots to support it. The

branches in their fall crushed all who were beneath them.
Falsehood escaped with an injured eye and broken leg,
which left him lame and squinting; which was coming off
cheaply.

Truth, suddenly restored to light, rose from the ground with
dishevelled hair and a stern countenance, and began harshly
to rebuke those about her for their weakness and credulity.

No sooner had he heard her voice than Falsehood cried,
"Behold the author of all our ills; the one who has de-
stroyed us. Death to her!" Upon which the people, armed
with sticks and stones, gave chase to the unhappy woman,
and thrust her again into the hole, more dead than alive.

Having done this, they quickly sealed it with a large stone, that Truth might never more arise from her tomb.

However, she had still a few friends ; for during the night an unknown hand traced the following epitaph upon the stone :

" Aqui yazé la Verdad,
    A quein el mundo cruel
    Mato sin enfermedad
    Porque no reinase en el
    Sino Mentira y Maldad."

Or, "Here lies Truth, slain not by disease, but by the cruel world, that nought might reign in it but Falsehood and Disloyalty."

It is Falsehood's smallest fault not to suffer contradiction. The friend of Truth was hunted down, and hung as soon as

found. Dead men only never grumble. To be better assured of his victory, Falsehood built him a palace over the sepulchre of Truth. But it is said that sometimes she turns in her grave, and thereupon the palace crumbles like a house of cards, and buries beneath its ruins all who dwell therein, both innocent and guilty.

But men have something else to do than mourn their dead ; they fall heirs to their inheritance. The people, those eternal dupes, each time rebuild the palace with greater splendor than before, and Falsehood, lame and squinting, reigns therein to this very day.

15

THE MYSTIC GARDEN.

A HEBREW APOLOGUE.

"REMEMBER the days of old, consider the years of many generations: ask thy father, and he will shew thee; thy elders, and they will tell thee."

If ever a people remained faithful to tradition it has been the Jewish people, to whom these words were addressed. It has preserved everything, history and legends, and, to be just, let us add that, the Bible excepted, it has jumbled them all up together. For this reason lovers of fairy lore have a weakness for this unhappy race, that has so long been the sport of fate and the scorn of nations. It has hoarded up for us the traditions of the East, and has borne and disseminated them through every quarter of the globe. Its spirit lives in us more than we are aware.

We are too ignorant how great has been the influence of the persecuted rabbis. Their books have been almost as much despised as themselves; yet they have been drawn upon largely. When we read an ingenious moral tale or a transparent apologue, we trouble ourselves little about the source from which it came; it is a kind of ingratitude which we commit every day, and for which we suffer little remorse.

Here is a story bequeathed us by the rabbis, which, though very old, deserves to be held in everlasting remembrance.

Once upon a time there lived a king who was exceeding mighty, sage, and just. This monarch caused a law to be proclaimed throughout his dominions, decreeing that no rewards, offices, or honors should be bestowed on any who had not merited them by services rendered their king or country, and that each should be rewarded according to his deserts.

In the course of time there were born at the court three children, all of royal blood. All three grew up richly endowed with virtue and talent—handsome, well-made, amiable, and beloved and esteemed by every one. The king, who was very fond of them, and was anxious to give them a station in accordance with their merit, called them to him one day, and said, "My children, I wish to do you the greatest possible honor and good. I would like to set you above all others in my palace, for you have found favor in my sight, and I believe you capable of the highest deeds of virtue. But all my people know, and you know with them, that there is a law in my kingdom which I cannot break. I can confer honors and office on no one, save as a reward for services that he has done. You cannot attain the high rank for which I destine you, therefore, by remaining at court. I advise you to go out into the world, scour the country far and wide, and try to win, by your exploits, the prize promised you by the law, and which I shall delight to bestow upon you. At

my summons, you will return to court ; until then, mark well
what you do ; for, according to your merit, such will be your
reward."

The three young men were very loath to quit the court,
but the king had ordered it, and they were forced to obey.
All three, therefore, took leave of their sovereign, and em-
barked in fine weather, leaving it to chance to shape their
course.

They had sailed a long way, when they spied an island
which looked fertile and smiling from the sea.   They landed, and found in the middle of the isle a fair garden full
of fruit.   As they drew near it, three guards came out to

"Three guards came out to meet them."

meet them, who permitted them to enter, but each gave them a word of advice.

The first guard told them that they must not expect to stay forever in this garden. The time would come when they would be forced to depart. None of those who had lived there before them had ever been allowed to remain. Such was the rule ; some came and others went.

The second guard bade them engrave it upon their memory that they must quit this garden precisely as they had entered it. They were free to enjoy all that they found there, and no one would hinder them ; but, on leaving, they were expressly forbidden to carry anything away with them.

The third guard advised them to be moderate in their enjoyments and pleasures, and to do nothing but what was virtuous and upright, adding, that this conduct would do much towards prolonging their lives.

Having heard these wise counsels, the youths entered the garden, which was even more beautiful and enchanting than it had seemed from outside. They found an abundance of trees laden with rich fruit, and plants and flowers as pleasing to the smell as to the sight. Nightingales were warbling in the branches of the huge oaks, myriads of birds delighted the ear with their melodious songs, and running streams diffused freshness and life everywhere.

It is needless to tell how great was the joy of the three comrades. They ate of the delicious fruits, drank of the sweet waters, and reposed under the leafy shade of the great trees, listening to the nightingales, while the gentle breeze wafted through the foliage the sweet odor of the flowers.

After a little while they parted, and each went his way to the part of the garden that pleased him best.

Fascinated by the beauty of the fruit and the coolness of the waters, the first of the three youths thought only of enjoying what lay nearest at hand. To eat, drink, sleep, lead a merry life, and cast away all care, such was his sole idea. He wholly forgot the counsels of the third guard.

The second of the young men was charmed neither by the fruit nor the flowers. He had found gold, silver, and precious stones in abundance in a corner of the garden. Dazzled by these treasures, he thought only of amassing them, and made his clothes into bags to hold all these riches. Absorbed in this idea, he neither ate, drank, nor slept. As to using the garden and its pleasures, he did not dream of it for a moment, forgetting what the second guard had told him, that whatever was found there must be enjoyed, and not hoarded, for nothing could be carried away with him.

The third youth had engraved upon his memory all that

"It is needless to tell how great was the joy of the three comrades."

the three guards had told him, and did not follow his companions' example. The course that they had pursued seemed to him dangerous and wrong; it was not what they had been taught to do. He made use of the garden and its pleasures, but only so far as was needful to sustain life. He passed his time in studying this abode, and what it contained. On beholding the fruits, flowers, and animals, with their prodigious diversity, and seeking

15*

the property of each plant, he marvelled at the perpetual miracle of nature; and on following the watercourses, so well distributed that, from step to step, and from ridge to ridge, there was not a blade of grass that was not watered, he never tired of contemplating the incredible order that set everything in its place.

What added to his astonishment was that, in this well-regulated garden, no gardener was to be seen. But reflection soon told him that order so perfect could not exist through accident, and that there must surely be a most wise gardener — an invisible master — who ruled this beautiful domain. Each day heightened his admiration; each day increased his desire to know the master of the garden; he sought him everywhere, and, without ever seeing him, he loved him for all the pleasure he had enjoyed in the sight and study of so many marvels.

While each of the young men was enjoying himself in his own fashion, a slave of the king brought them a summons to return at once to court and give an account of their life.

They set out for the gate by which they had entered, but scarcely had he passed it, when the first of the three— he who had thought only of his pleasure—grew faint from the change of air, and, no longer having the fruit of the garden to sustain him, his body puffed up, his strength failed him, and he fell on the ground and expired.

The second one dragged himself slowly along, laden like

a pack-mule. The hope of one day enjoying his treasure made him forget his fatigue; but, on reaching the gate of the garden, the guards, astonished at seeing him move so heavily, laid hold of him, and stripped him in an instant of all his spoil. The unhappy youth groaned and wept; all his pains and labor had led to nothing but wretchedness and despair.

The third youth had felt a lively joy on hearing the voice of the messenger who summoned him by order of the king. The master whom he had been unable to see, he should doubtless find on quitting the garden, and could express to him all his love and gratitude. Moreover, he had committed no offence; far from it; he had done everything to recognize his will and to obey him. It was, therefore, with a heart full of hope, and without a thought of what he left behind him, that he ran to the garden gate. He was warmly welcomed by the guards, who rejoiced to see the alacrity with which he obeyed the king's commands.

On drawing near the court, the youth who had been stripped of his booty was so weary and miserable that he could scarcely keep his feet. It was in vain that he insisted that he was of royal blood; no one believed him; still more, the slaves

of the palace, indignant that such a beggar should claim relationship with the king, turned him from the palace door, and threw him into a narrow dungeon, where he would have full time to expiate his faults and bewail his folly.

The third youth was as royally welcomed as his comrade was harshly treated. All the grandees of the court went out to meet him, embraced him, and accompanied him to the king's presence to do him honor. The king was greatly rejoiced to see this young man, so alert and ready to do his bidding, and although nothing was hidden from his knowledge, he asked the new-comer what he had done since he saw him last. The youth told the story of all the great and beautiful things he had seen in the delicious place where he had been, and added: "I am quite sure that this garden has a master of exceeding great wisdom; this master cannot be far off, though he takes delight in hiding himself from our sight; and it is my chief desire to express to him the love and gratitude I have felt at the sight of his works."

"Since your time has been so well spent, I will grant your wish," answered the king. "I am the master of yonder garden; I rule it from here through the ministers of my will; and there is not a creature so small, or a blade of grass so humble, that it has not a servant to cherish it and watch its growth."

On hearing these words, and comprehending this mystery, the happy youth felt his love for his master glow still brighter in his breast; he tasted infinite joy in the knowledge of his power, and dwelt forevermore side by side with him at the court, raised to the highest pinnacle of honor.

The moral of this story, continue the rabbis, is easily discerned. The king is the supreme Creator and Sovereign Ruler of all things. The garden is the world; the three youths represent the three kinds of men that are here on earth; one seeks nothing but pleasure; the second pursues fortune, and the third loves goodness alone, which is the true aim of man. That the three young men are of royal blood signifies that they belong to Israel, the chosen people of God. As to the counsels of the three guards, we know that they are true. The first is God's own words to Adam, "Dust thou art, and to dust shalt thou return." The second is the saying of Job, "Naked came I out of my mother's womb, and naked shall I return thither." Lastly, the third is the great speech of Moses, our master in Israel, appointed by God : " I have set before thee this day life and good, and death and evil. Therefore choose life, that both thou and thy seed may live."

Does not this signify that life consists in doing good, and death in doing evil?

He who weighs well these three sayings, and always bears them in mind, cannot mistake the true path, but will find the road which, on quitting life, leads to everlasting repose. Keep this example, therefore, before thine eyes like a mirror. And now, in his infinite mercy, may God grant thee grace to serve him, and may'st thou in this manner obtain peace in this life, and glory in the life to come. Amen.

THE EVE
OF
ST. MARK.

AN ESTHONIAN
FAIRY TALE.

I.

NEAR Revel, in Esthonia, on the shores of the Gulf of Finland, there once lived an old sorcerer, who had thoroughly mastered all the secrets of the black art. He knew everything, saw everything, understood everything, and could do everything. To turn dust into gold, or gold into dust, to assemble the winds, summon or quell the tempest, hush the thunders, or call the dead from their graves—all this was to him but child's play. He held earth, sea, and air at his bidding. It was a common saying concerning him, that the sun and moon trembled at his sight, lest he should send them to shine upon a world even wick-

eder than ours. The devil himself, with all his pride and cunning, was nought but a slave before this terrible magician.

In spite of all his knowledge, might, and wealth, our hero

was not hap-
py. Although he
harmed nobody,
and willingly showed kindness to the poor, he was
detested and shunned by
all. When he entered a
village the women fled with
their children in their arms,
and the men shut them-

selves up in their houses till he went by. The only ones who remained in the streets were those who had some favor to ask ; they bowed to the ground and kissed his hand, as if he had been a lord ; but no sooner had he turned his back than they cursed him in their hearts, or shook their fists after him. It is the penalty of omnipotence to be loved by no one, and to have your footsteps dogged by envy, malice, and ingratitude.

Our magician had had a sad experience. When young he had sought to marry; but, in spite of his knowledge and power, no one had been willing to accept him as a suitor. A woman does not like to have her heart always laid bare, and no girl is so young as not to know that it is the first requisite of a good husband that he should not be a sorcerer. The poor man lived alone, therefore, in an old Gothic manorhouse, with a great dog and a black cat for his sole companions. With the first he talked politics, and philosophized with the second. Let no one be surprised to see a feline philosopher ; it was long ago acknowledged by sages that the finest systems of metaphysics are nought but pap for cats.

One stormy day, our sorcerer amused himself by walking upon the raging waters. The whistling wind, rumbling thunder, and dashing breakers helped him to forget his sad thoughts. Suddenly, by the flash of the lightning, he saw a sinking ship, upon whose deck lay an infant in its cradle. To snatch the innocent victim from death, and bear it away in his arms, was the work of an instant. The waves had not closed over the vessel before the old man was in his house, lulling with ineffable tenderness the child, who gazed in his face without fear. It was the first time that any human being had smiled upon him. The dog licked the tiny feet of the new-comer, happy to share in his master's joy, while the cat, with sphinx-like gravity, fixed his green eyes upon the stranger, as if about to ask him some riddle, and devour him if it was not solved.

In this solitude, far from towns and men, the orphan grew up among the three friends by whom he had been adopted. Adolf, as he was named by the sorcerer, was no common child, and profited well by the lessons of his masters. The magician taught him the language of birds and beasts; the dog showed him how to be gentle, patient, kind, and good; as to the cat, it was by means of his claws that he inducted into his flesh and spirit the first principle of all morality, "Do not scratch others, if you wish them to leave you with a whole skin."

For sixteen years Adolf lived happily with his father. He could not take a step in the great forests that surrounded the old manor, without meeting friends and comrades. He gambolled with the doe's fawns around their mother; he played hot cockles with the bear cubs, and hide-and-seek with the rabbits; the ever-anxious hare confided to him her cares and troubles, and the squirrel taught him how to climb the trees and pick the plumpest nuts. The lark, linnet, and thrush warbled their sweetest songs at his approach. Together they leaped, sang, and made such an uproar that some owl, disturbed in his slumbers, would come, with his round eyes and hooked beak, gravely to preach that the day was made for sleep, and that stagnation was wisdom. You should have seen how the troop of madcaps greeted the poor fool, and what a noise they made when he returned to his hole in despair, carrying with him his hooting and sermonizing.

In this way Adolf passed his days, knowing neither sorrow nor care. When he returned home at night, with sparkling eyes and flowing locks, the sorcerer never tired of listening to and admiring him. To spare him a tear, he would have laid at his feet all his learning and treasures. It is the privi-

DESSIN PAR H.PILLE   EAU-FORTE DE H.MANESSE

"The dog licked the tiny feet of the new-comer, happy to share in his
master's joy."

lege of youth to be loved—an inestimable blessing, of whose
value it is ignorant; as for old age, its only joy is in loving
and being happy in the happiness of others.

Unhappily, in the forests as in the town, evil tongues are
always found, that meddle with what does not concern them.
That gossip, the magpie, that goes prowling about, peering
into everything, and that can keep neither her eyes nor her
beak to herself, had no sooner spied the handsome Adolf
than she asked him, with a pitying air, why he lived alone
in the woods like a wolf.　Revel was only six leagues away;
why did he not go to see the walls, towers, castle, and bell
of the ancient city of Waldemar?　"It is true," she added,
in her jargon, " that the thrushes are coquettish dames who
chatter all the time, but what are they in comparison with
the fine city belles who change their plumage and their tune
every day?　Then there are the men at the tavern at night,
with their songs, laughter, noise, and jollity.　He who has

not seen all this has lived with his eyes shut.   People vegetate in the woods ; they live only in the city."

Saying this, the magpie shook her tail, cocked up her head, and called on a sparrow who had come from Revel that morning to munch cherries, to prove her words.   Friquet, a true cit, a bold glutton and impudent braggart, screeched in his shrillest tones that it was the most shameful thing in the world for any one but a beast to live in the woods. "Hurrah for the town !" he cried ; "where men drink when they are not thirsty, eat when they are not hungry, and amuse themselves by doing nothing. They turn  day into night there, and winter into summer ; it is the land of pleasure and liberty.   To bury one's self in the country when one is young, rich, and handsome, is stupid, foolish, and wicked."

"Unless," added Margot, the magpie, "there are those who selfishly keep you at home, knowing that in the town they would have to share their treasure with delightful men and lovely women.   Farewell, my dear Adolf, you are a good little boy, and your papa ought to be very much pleased with you.   Come, Friquet, there are some charming people expecting us in town ; we must not tire them with waiting ; how could they dine without us?"

The silly talk of these feather-brained gossips threw poor Adolf into strange confusion. It was in vain that his friends the birds sang him their merriest songs, and that the rabbit

tried to amuse him with his tricks and antics; the forest seemed a desert. At the corner of each path he looked for a human figure; he felt the need of mingling with beings like himself, whom he had never seen except in books and pictures. Weary with this vain desire, he returned home with hanging head and dejected mien. For the first time in his life he felt unhappy.

Scarcely had he let himself drop upon a seat when Cæsar, the dog, looked at him with anxious eyes.

"Adolf," said he, "something is the matter with you."

The child stroked the dog and did not answer.

Mustache, the cat, who was asleep under the stove, half opened one eye, and pricked up his ears.

"Adolf," said he, "something is the matter with you."

Adolf sighed, and did not answer.

The sorcerer, who had been listening, drew from his girdle a little mirror in which he could read men's thoughts. Scarcely had he cast his eyes on it when he turned pale.

"Adolf," he murmured, in a trembling voice, "you wish to leave us."

"To leave you, father!" cried the child; "never! I am so happy with you."

And he burst into tears.

"My child," said the sorcerer, "I read your soul better than you can yourself. You are tired of staying here; you wish to go to the city, and live with men. I had planned for you a happier lot. I wished to keep you with me, and to spare you the bitterness and deceptions of life. But man cannot escape his fate. Go where your heart calls you; to-morrow you shall set out for the city."

"With you, father?"

"No, my son; at my age and with my experience, solitude alone is endurable. But you shall not go alone; I will give you companions that will watch over you."

Adolf, threw himself, weeping, into his father's arms, and vowed he would never leave him. The sorcerer embraced him, and smiled mournfully. An hour later, Adolf was asleep and sweetly dreaming, while the old man sat on the foot of the bed and gazed at the child through his tears.

II.

At sunrise Adolf was ready to go. Three black horses stood in waiting at the castle gate. The handsomest and most spirited was for him; the others were held by two imposing-looking squires; one, dressed in white, with a cocked hat on his head, was none other than honest Cæsar, turned into a valet; while the other, in black, with a knife thrust in his belt, was easily recognized, by his grimace, as Mustache, with his green eyes, and thick, bristling coat.

There is nothing so sad as parting. Once on the road, the three friends proceeded a long way in silence. But by degrees the sun rose in the heavens, their tongues were loosened, and they chattered as merrily as birds. Cæsar admired all Adolf's madcap speeches, for he loved him; Mustache grumbled unceasingly, and admired nothing in the world but himself—he was a philosopher.

Laughing and disputing, they passed through the forest, and came to the turn of the road where it entered the plain, when Adolf cried out, pointing to his companions a strange figure, at which he shuddered. By the side of the road, leaning with both hands on a crutch, and shaking all over, was an old woman, in rags. Her uncombed gray locks fell dishevelled about her wrinkled, yellow face; her dim eyes were almost hidden under her inflamed eyelids; her hooked nose and sharp, turned-up chin nearly met, like the beaks of two fighting-cocks, and her mouth, with its toothless gums, babbled confused sounds.

"What is this?" asked Adolf.

" A gypsy, a beggar, a thief," said Mustache.

"A poor woman bowed down with old age," said Cæsar.

"What is old age?" asked Adolf, who had never seen anything like this in the forest.

"Old age," answered the sententious Mustache, "is the winter of life. When the snow falls, the trees shed their leaves; when the hair turns white, man sheds his teeth, eyes, stomach, and legs. It is the law of nature."

"And I shall soon be like this poor creature," sighed Adolf.

"No, my son," returned Cæsar. "It takes seventy or eighty years to make an old man of a child, and you are only sixteen."

"Seventy years soon pass," exclaimed Mustache. "As the great poet Pindar sings, 'Life is the dream of a shadow.' An admirable saying for a personage who was neither a cat nor a philosopher by trade."

By Cæsar's advice, Adolf flung some money to the old woman, then spurred on his horse to escape this mournful spectacle. They rode fast, moreover, for they were beginning to be hungry, like mere mortals, and they spied in the distance the smoke of a village. "At last," thought Adolf, "I shall behold mankind."

The first house that they came to was a decent-looking inn, with a golden lion for a sign. They called, but no one answered. The door stood half-way open ; they entered the public room, and knocked with their whips on the table. Suddenly, they heard a groan in an adjoining chamber. Adolf ran to answer the plaintive call, and found himself face to face with a new kind of misery.

Upon a mattress on the floor lay a young woman with two children in her arms, one shaking with chills, and the other burning with fever. The poor hollow-eyed mother could only stammer a few words with her parched lips.

"Pardon me, good sirs," said she, "we have the spring fever ; this is the day of the chills, and I am not able to wait on you."

"Is there not another inn in the village?" asked Mustache.

"Yes, but do not go there, good sir. Small-pox is raging in it just now. The best thing for you to do is to hasten to Revel, for our village is full of the epidemic. Excuse me, and may God be with you !"

"Is there nothing I can do for you?" cried Adolf.

"Thank you, my lord," answered she; "time is the only cure for the sickness sent by Heaven. We must be resigned."

Once out of this gloomy abode, Adolf turned to Mustache.

"What is sickness?" asked he. "I never saw anything
of the kind among the companions of my solitude."

"In truth," returned the green-eyed philosopher, "sickness
is the monopoly of man : he alone has fevers and physicians."

"Are people often ill?" asked Adolf.

"That depends upon temperaments," replied Mustache ;
"women are ill all their lives, or think that they are, which
amounts to the same thing. As to men, the healthiest suf-

fer little except during childhood, old age, and a part of middle life."

"It is frightful!" cried the youth.

"Bah!" replied the philosopher, "it is the law of human nature. As yonder woman said, with excellent judgment, we must be resigned."

"Poor creatures!" thought Adolf. "Menaced with sickness and old age, how you must cling together, and help and love each other!"

"Look yonder, master!" exclaimed Cæsar.

Adolf raised his eyes and saw a crowd of peasants, seated around tables set along the road. Each one held a mug or bottle in his hand; some were singing and others shouting. One was dancing on the table amid the clattering glasses, while his companions kept time with him by drumming on the wood with their knives.

"What is that?" asked Adolf.

"A village festival," answered Cæsar.

"Happy men!" sneered Mustache; "drunk and crazy!"

"At last," said Adolf, "we have found people who enjoy life."

As he was speaking, some soldiers marched along the highway, and were hailed by the revellers. One of them answered with an oath, whereupon a bottle was flung at his head. He stooped in time to avoid the blow, and picked up a huge stone, which he hurled among the crowd. A sharp cry was heard; the stone had struck a woman full in the face, and the blood was trickling down her cheeks. At the sight, the drunken men fell in a body upon the soldiers, arming themselves with whatever came to hand—bottles, jugs, benches, and sticks. The soldiers drew their swords in self-defence, and a sharp conflict followed, which, however, was of short duration.

Before Adolf could reach the field of battle, two of the

soldiers, followed by volleys of stones, were fleeing towards the
town, loudly calling for help, and leaving their comrades on
the ground, lifeless or writhing in death.   They were avenged,
however, for side by side with them lay three dead and several dying peasants, while others were carried off by their
comrades, who stanched their wounds while trying to escape
before the soldiers returned.   The men were sullen and

angry ; the women shrieking and the children crying ; it was
a heart-rending sight.

Adolf threw himself on his knees by the side of a peasant
who had been ripped open by a sabre thrust, and was wrapped
in eternal slumber, and tried to question his sightless eyes
and speechless lips.

" What is this ?" asked he of Cæsar.

" Alas, master," was the answer, " it is death. This man's
sufferings are over ; he will never more awake."

" Yes," said Mustache, " life is a dream that begins and
ends in nothingness. Dust before birth, and dust after death·
Such are man and his destiny."

" What !" exclaimed Adolf, " is life so easily lost, and yet do
men so little respect this precious possession of their fellows?"

" Bah !" said Mustache, " their greatest pleasure is to kill
each other. Nations hold in remembrance none but the con-
querors who slay them. Fame is bloodshed."

" My friends," cried the youth, " let us return to my father.
I will not go to Revel. As for men, I have seen too much
of them ; my heart is broken. Take me back to our forests,
and let me forget the terrible lesson I have had to-day."

III.

On hearing these words, Mustache smiled grimly to himself, and hastily turned back towards the manor. Cæsar
tried to comfort Adolf, but the youth hung his head and paid
no heed to him. He was crushed with grief, and his heart
was overflowing with bitterness. He was tired of men, but
solitude appalled him. On the word of two chattering birds,
he had pictured to himself a world full of enchantment ; he
had had a delightful dream, and at sixteen it is not easy to
renounce these sweet illusions.

While Cæsar and Mustache galloped on, each seeking to

be the first to tell the sorcerer of his child's return, Adolf pensively followed the path that he had trodden so gayly in the morning. Night was falling, and the shadows deepened his sadness.

"What is the matter, Adolf?" murmured a gentle voice. "Has anything gone wrong with you?"

The youth raised his head, and saw a nightingale perched upon a twig.

"Good-evening, dear bird," said he, "why are you not singing as usual? Is your heart wrung like mine? Perhaps you too have seen mankind?"

"No," answered the nightingale, "I am not singing to-night, because I am saving myself for a great occasion. This is the eve of St. Mark; and I am keeping my voice to serenade the one I love."

"Alas!" said Adolf, "she whom you love cannot escape sickness, old age, or death."

"What are you thinking of?" returned the nightingale; "the fairies of the night are immortal; their youth and beauty never fade."

"Are they good?" asked the youth.

"They are goodness itself. Their hearts are full of pity for all who suffer here below."

"I must see them," cried Adolf.

"My handsome friend," said the nightingale, "they are only to be seen once a year, on the eve of St. Mark, and to reach their dwelling without danger, you must have wings."

"Oh, nightingale, dear nightingale," cried the youth, "take me with you. Show me the way to them. Do not refuse me, if you love me."

"My child," returned the nightingale, "I fear I have talked too much. We birds have more feathers than brains. Forget my gossiping, and forgive me."

But Adolf insisted so warmly, and with so many prayers and tears, that the nightingale said, shaking his head,

"My child, my child, there is danger in knowing too much. Many things are hid from man's eyes for his happiness. If ever you see the fairies, farewell to your peace of mind; the world that delights you will be nought but a desert, and you will pass your life in regretting a vanished dream."

"No, no, dear bird," cried the youth; "away with this mistaken pity. If I do not see the fairies this night, nothing is left me but to die. Grant my prayer, and save my life."

"If that is so," said the nightingale, "I will tell you what to do; but the danger is great and the success doubtful.

"Know, then, that every year, on the eve of St. Mark, at midnight, the King of the Serpents holds high court in the great marsh where the water-lilies grow. A golden cup, filled with the milk of the goats of the sky, is then offered him. If you can seize the cup and drink a draught of this magic milk, your eyes will be opened, and you will see all that night hides with its sable cloak from the eyes of mortals. But remember that all the serpents in the world will be at this meeting, and that one of their bites will kill you."

"They cannot be worse than men," rejoined Adolf, "and, besides, what have I to fear from death? I have lost all relish for life."

And with these words he leaped from his horse, threw the reins on its neck, and plunged into the forest.

IV.

When Adolf reached the great water-lily marsh after a long walk, he found nothing there but silence and darkness. Although it was spring, he thought he saw by the light of the stars that the grass had just been cut. Piles of new-mown hay were lying here and there, as in harvest-time, otherwise all was unchanged; nothing was stirring, and our hero began to think that a trick had been played on him, when a distant clock slowly struck midnight. Immediately a strange light appeared in the midst of the marsh, looking like a star fallen from heaven. Adolf approached this apparition, when the turf around him seemed crawling like an ant-hill. What he had taken for heaps of grass were thousands of serpents asleep on the ground, that had awakened at the summons of their lord and were hastening to pay him homage.

The youth's surprise may well be imagined, but it was too late to draw back. All that he could do was to keep in the shade, and follow this multitude, crawling silently onward. Ere long, he saw an enormous dragon, wearing on its head a crown of emeralds and rubies, the lustre of which lighted

" When Adolf reached the great water-lily marsh, he found **nothing**
there but silence and darkness."

the forest afar off. It was his majesty, the King of the Serpents. Around him, like courtiers vying with each other for the smile of their prince, thronged adders, asps, vipers, and serpents of all sizes and colors, entangled together, all stretching up their turgid necks, and darting out their forked tongues, hissing loudly. The noise was deafening, and the sight one that might have frozen the boldest heart with terror.

We would not venture to say that our hero was not frightened; but at the sight of the golden cup he forgot his terror. Without thinking of danger, he threw himself like a madman into this host of serpents, more numerous and closely serried than the blades of grain in a wheat-field, rushed to the cup, seized it, drained it at a draught, and flung it far from him. Then, feeling escape impossible, he folded his arms, and awaited death.

To his great joy, however, the dragon snatched the cup and fled with it. The whole army of serpents followed their chief with frightful hisses. Adolf found himself alone in the forest, where all again was silent. His heart had not yet ceased to throb loudly, when he heard the first notes of the nightingale. The bird had not deceived him; the fairies were coming.

V.

The moon rose, illumining the forest with its silver light. Our hero looked around him. The marsh was transformed into a glade carpeted with moss; the trees were covered with leaves, and violets were blossoming everywhere. In the distance, Adolf caught glimpses of light figures flitting through the forest like sylphs floating over the turf.

There was no more doubt, they were the fairies of the night. How beautiful they were, in their white drapery, clasped on one shoulder, their hair carelessly knotted be-

"They skimmed over the moss without touching it."

hind, and their arms and feet bare, as they skimmed over the moss without touching it!

On reaching the place of rendezvous, each was eagerly questioned by her companions. Adolf listened with delight to the soft murmur of their voices, sweeter than the babbling of the forest brooks.

"Where have you been, sister, where have you been?"

"I have been to the red house, where poor old Bridget had fallen asleep over her spinning-wheel, exhausted with toil, and forgetting that she would have no bread for to-morrow if her task was not done. I sat in her lap, took her distaff in my hand, turned her wheel, and spun thread enough for a whole week."

"Where have you been, sister ; where have you been ?"

" I have been to the little cabin by the sea-shore, where a poor woman has been waiting for a year for her husband to come home from sea. Yesterday I spied his ship off the coast; I showed him to her in a dream, smiling, and saying, 'Patience, dear love, in three days I will be in your arms.' "

"Where have you been, sister ; where have you been ?"

" I have been to the shop of Harold, the money-lender. For three nights past I have scratched on the wall like a mouse, and cried in his ear, ' Look to your treasure, the robbers are here ! ' He shall not sleep who shows no pity to the poor."

"Where have you been, sister ; where have you been ?"

" I have been to the cottage of Wilhelm, the gamekeeper. The poor man lost his wife nine months ago, and when he makes his rounds at night, the house is left alone. I found the baby crying, and about to fall from its bed. I took it in my arms and sung it a lullaby, upon which it smiled at me as if I had been its mother, and fell asleep."

"Where have you been, sister ; where have you been ?"

"I have been to the house of the rich Gustaf, who has no mercy on his tenants. I found him snoring in an arm-chair, drunk with wine and his newly-gotten wealth. I set all the candles ablaze, upon which he tumbled on the floor in af-fright, crying ' Fire !' Let his castle burn ; it will teach him that the great have need of the small here below."

"Where have you been, sister ; where have you been ?"

" I have been to the green cottage, where Matilda is mourn-ing the loss of her child. I gave it back to her in a dream, and she will hold it in her arms until daybreak. When she

awakes, she will doubtless weep; but she will know that her
child is still living in the unseen world, and hope will spring
up anew in her heart."

At this moment the nightingale greeted the moon at the
zenith with his sweetest song. The fairies joined hands in
a circle, and danced around, singing, in low tones,

" When summer days die,
  All who breathe, all who sigh,
  Come under our sceptre,
    The dark world we keep.
  Then mortals, poor children,
  Wake not nor weep,
  Sleep, all of you, sleep;
  We will watch over you,
    Watch we will keep!

" Silence rules the vast land
  While we dance, hand in hand,
  And through the dance murmur
    Our songs soft and deep.
  Then mortals, poor children,
  Wake not nor weep,
  Sleep, all of you, sleep;
  We will watch over you,
    Watch we will keep."

The round finished, the fairies separated into different
groups. Some seated themselves on the grass, and gathered
the violets, primroses, and white strawberry blossoms that
grew about them; while others danced in couples, to the
music of their companions' song:

" We are the voices,
  And all the sweet noises,
    Of the wind in the tree;
  And where perfumes and shadows
  Chase over the meadows,
    The zephyrs are we.

" We are the lightning
That, darkling and brightening,
Furrows all the thick night.
And the marsh fires we are,
That, glancing afar,
Shake the shepherd with fright.

" In the starbeam that nightly
Some great sail leads lightly
O'er the bitter, salt wave,
Our torches are burning,
To clear lustre turning
Seas dark as the grave.

" In bell tones whose sweetness
Clangs out day's completeness
We dwell with delight;
We the plash of the stream,
And we, too, the dream
That is born of the night.

" We, murmurs eternal,
We, whispers supernal,
We, smiles of the skies,
Charm all sadness away
From a world far too gray,
Far too old, far too wise!"

Intoxicated by these magic songs and dances, Adolf, forgetting all prudence, quitted his retreat and approached the fairies. One of them—the most graceful of all—passed so near him that she touched him with her dress. Adolf madly seized her hand. The fairy turned round sharply, but sadly smiled on seeing the trembling youth.

" Poor child," she murmured, " you would have it so."

Leaving her hand in Adolf's, she looked at him, burst into tears, and kissed his forehead. He felt a thrill run through his veins, and swooned away.

VI.

When he regained consciousness, the sun was high in the heavens. He looked around him with astonishment. On his left was Cæsar, trying to warm him with his breath; on his right sat Mustache, washing his own face.

"Imprudent boy," cried Cæsar, "why did you stay so late on the marsh? The night cold has chilled you through. If you knew how anxious your father is about you!"

"Cæsar, my good Cæsar," exclaimed Adolf, "where are the fairies? I must see them again."

"He is raving," said the grave Mustache. "Just as I expected. It is the effort of nature to bring back the warmth by an increase of the vital force."

"Mustache," cried Adolf, "where are the fairies? I have seen them; I must see them again."

"What fairies?"

"The fairies of the night; the invisible ones."

"How can you see what is invisible?" returned the cat; "the idea is unphilosophical."

"Cæsar, my friend," said Adolf, "let us return to my father; he alone can understand my trouble."

"I will run and tell my master to send some way of carrying you home," exclaimed Mustache; "for, judging by your pale face, my poor boy, you are not able to set one foot before the other.

If you had had the wisdom to listen to my lessons in philosophy, you would never have lost yourself in the woods, chasing a will-o'-the-wisp ; you would have—"

"Adolf," said Cæsar, "put your arms round my neck, and try to climb on my back, as you used to do when a child. Perhaps I shall have strength enough to carry you home."

It was in this style that our hero returned to the old manor, and was deposited in the sorcerer's great arm-chair. His father felt very much like scolding him, but was seized with deep anxiety on seeing him so trembling and dejected.

"What is the matter, my son?" cried he, folding him in his arms.

"Father, where are the fairies? I have seen them, and I must see them again."

"Curses on them!" cried the sorcerer ; "they have stolen away my child! My dear Adolf, ask anything my art can procure. Would you have gold? I will make you so rich that men will grovel on their knees before you and kiss the ground you tread on. Are you ambitious? I will give you a kingdom ; twenty of them, if you like. You shall be surrounded with smiling faces ; men shall applaud all your whims, and women shall crowd around you to win a glance from your eyes. The world is mine ; it shall be yours ; I lay it at your feet ; but my power does not extend beyond this world ; do not ask me for what belongs to another."

"Father, I want but one thing—again to see the invisible fairies."

"Alas!" cried the sorcerer, "of what use is all my power and knowledge? The heart of a child has desires that the empire of the world will not satisfy."

"Father!" cried the youth, "I see them! I hear them!

Listen to the heavenly melodies." And he murmured in a faint voice :

> " Then mortals, poor children,
> Wake not nor weep.
> Sleep, all of you, sleep ;
> We will watch over you,
> Watch we will keep !"

" Adolf, my child, be yourself again !" cried the old man, pressing his son to his heart.

" Look, father, she is there ! Do you see her? She smiles on me ; she calls me ! This time, she herself stretches out her hand to me. ' Poor child !' she says, 'you would have it so.' Yes, I would indeed. Oh, fairies, my sisters, I cannot live without you. Wait for me ; I am coming, I am coming !"

A smile flitted over his pale face, he stretched out his arms and tried to rise, then his head fell back in the chair, and all was over.

VII.

The old manor has long been in ruins. The ivy has invaded everything, even to the dilapidated roof, and a great oak has pushed its boughs through the front steps. For more than a century this gloomy abode has been inhabited only by flocks of ravens, with here and there a solitary osprey ; yet the peasants never willingly pass its abandoned walls after nightfall. It is said that groans are heard to issue from the turrets at night, and that fiery eyes blaze there through the darkness. The sorcerer is not forgotten, and at evening, when the doors are closed, men still talk of Adolf and the fairies whose sight was death to him. Whether this is history or legend, he would be bold, indeed, who would venture to aver. The sages of our day believe only in what

they can see or touch.   For my part, not being a sage, all
that a long life has taught me is that there is nothing true in
this world but what we do not see.   God grant that, like
Adolf, I may some day behold the unseen, were it only to
forget for a moment what I cannot avoid seeing here on
earth.